Not From Round Here
Memoirs of a Soft Southerner Up North

Bradley Chermside

ISBN: 9798879214550

In loving memory of Matthew Skirrow. They don't make them like you anymore Skiz x

Contents

Chapter 1

Stranger Danger

In Japan, it's socially acceptable to slurp out loud when eating noodles. In Greece, spitting on the bride is encouraged rather than frowned upon (symbolically, of course! Please don't actually launch a loogie at her). In Denmark, it's commonplace to picnic in a cemetery (better double-check those chocolate fingers!).

It is not normal, however, under any circumstances, to say hello to someone you don't know where I grew up down south. In my hometown of Basildon, Essex, we'd rather chew on a jellyfish than endure such social discomfort. We'll pretend we've got an itch – the crotch area is always best to put people off engaging with you. Cross the street. Make out we're talking on the phone, hoping someone doesn't actually ring. So when a complete stranger says hello at a bus stop in a random town soon after touching down up north at Manchester Airport, I don't quite know how to react.

'Morning!' a bespectacled little balding man says as he passes me shivering in the early autumn wind and rain.

'Al . . . alright, mate?' I stammer back, wondering what he could be scheming.

'Me?' he replies, hand on heart. 'I'm alright, it's t'others I'm worried about. See y'again,' he says ominously.

Leaning on my giant suitcase waiting for my connecting bus to take me to my in-laws' house, I wonder why on earth he said hello to me. Is he up to something? Still drunk from the Friday night before? Has he been let out for the day? What if he's forgotten to take his medication? What if he's taken too much of it, or worse still, escaped?

I reconnoitre the streets to check if he's coming back to "see me again." He's not, thank god, but danger is still present – there's another man coming along the pot-holed pavement towards me from the other direction. Perhaps he's an accomplice? Perhaps he's one of "the others" the man is worried about?

'You okay, pal?' the accomplice enquires in a gravelly, morning-after voice before taking a long drag on his vape, leaving the scent of strawberries suspended in the air.

'Great, thanks,' I reply, eyes narrowing in suspicion.

As he lollops off, passing a shuttered fish and chip shop called "Rock and a Hard Plaice", I have a flashback to when something similar happened in Camden, North London.

A hooded male said hello outside the tube station, then pestered me halfway up the high street going on about some bloke called "Charlie." Apparently, this Charlie had some "good gear" or something? I didn't need good gear then and I don't need it now. All I need is for my bus to arrive so I can get to my in-laws', completing my journey that began seven hours ago at dawn in Tenerife, where I'd been living pre-pandemic.

I dig out my phone and post on social media, hoping some of my friends of northern descent can help me out. Maybe they know something I don't?

"*People are speaking to me,*" I thumb into my phone like my life depends on it. "*Is this normal up north?*"

"*That's us!*" comes the first comment.

"*Welcome t'north!*" another chips in.

"*Won't be long before someone invites you in for a brew and biscuits,*" someone else promises.

Could they be right? Could it be that these are nothing more than pleasantries between strangers that may, one day, become brew and biscuit buddies? Is there really nothing more in it than that? No other expectations other than to exchange cheery sentiments and human warmth on a cold, wet and windy Saturday morning in September?

When my bus finally squeals to a halt and hisses open its doors to invite me in, I get another not-so-pleasant surprise – the driver needs the exact money. Which I don't have. Neither will his machine accept my Spanish bank card. Just as I'm expecting to be told to "Get off my bus you fackin' chancer," as had once happened in my hometown down south –

'No problem, pal,' the driver says, beckoning me aboard for a free ride. 'You're not from reauwnd 'ere, are you?' he asks with a curious tilt of the head.

'That obvious, it is?' I reply, making sure my face mask is correctly in place so I don't get into more trouble.

'You're like a cat amongst pigeons with that bloomin' thing on your 'ead,' he says, pointing at my West Ham hat.

'Oh yeah, sorry about that,' I apologise, then whip the hat bearing the badge of my beloved football team off my head before he changes his mind.

After thanking him more times than necessary and stopping just short of offering to stroke his arm hairs while he drives (my wife does this and I really like it – to me, I should stress, not to bus drivers), I take a seat where I'm being driven sideways. At a right angle, to my left, are two forward-facing ladies. The surplus amount of love they appear to be handling suggests they might have loyalty cards at Rock and a Hard Plaice. With their hands resting on their shopping trolleys in front of them, their many chins are wagging 10 to the dozen.

'Did you know I've got tattoo?' the first lady asks her friend.

'Have yer?'

'Yeah I have. At first, I were gonna get Barr-eh,' she says, rolling up a jacket sleeve to show where the letters might've been inked into her forearm. 'Like Barr-eh White.'

'I like Barry White,' her bus buddy replies.

'I just got "Mam" int' end.' The Barry White fan sighs, rolling over a wrist to show her.

'People tell me I look like Meryl Streak,' comes her friend's reply.

'It's actually Meryl Streep, and yeah, you do look a lot like her.'

I want to agree but daren't engage with them just in case they're in cahoots with "the others" who are coming to "see me again".

'So . . . where were I?' the Barry White fan rewinds.

'You were talking about bloke chatting you up,' says Meryl Streak, jogging her memory.

'Oh yeah, that were it. So, I turned around and says to him, "Me fanny's me own, leave it alone." And then he says, "I bet your fanny's like a cheese toasty. All sticky."'

'He didn't?!'

'He bloody did.'

'Bloody cheek of it!'

The Barry White lady catches me laughing under my breath.

'What must you think of us two,' she says.

'He probably thinks I'm your carer,' her mate cracks.

'She were past caring a long time ago,' the Barry White lady comes back.

I shyly smile back at them, then itch my crotch to put them off talking to me again.

After the double-decker bus has chugged, shuddered and bumped its way past fertile fields, car showrooms and retail parks, it throws its doors open at my stop.

Dragging my suitcase behind me through the sodden streets to my in-laws' where I'll spend the next two weeks in mandatory Covid quarantine due to my arrival from overseas, I wonder if I'll get more unexpected yet welcome pleasantries.

Lo and behold, it happens again – not once but three times! A pensioner with trousers tucked into his socks is pushing his bike into the driving rain when he says good morning. A dog walker says nothing but extends an arm and gives me a thumbs up, and a lady wrestling her umbrella with the wind points at my suitcase and asks me if I've been anywhere nice.

'A lot nicer than this,' I grumble, then make for a coffee shop with tables and chairs set out underneath an awning where I can take cover.

Standing under the awning and shaking raindrops off my West Ham hat, I take stock – that's five times in the hour or so since I touched down that a stranger has said hello. Five more times than ever happened in my two decades growing up on the outskirts of London. Five more times than ever happened in my 10 years living in Tenerife. People just don't do that in the places I've lived before moving here.

After messaging my wife to say I'd be there soon, I reflect on how this forced move up north could just turn out to be a blessing in disguise after all.

I was none too keen on returning to the UK from Tenerife where I'd spent the past 10 years working as a professional singer, bought an apartment and met my wife, Rachel, a fellow singer and entertainer. I'd got accustomed to Tenerife's sizzling, sub-Saharan climate, became fluent in Spanish and even learned the dance moves to the Macarena. No doubt about it, I'd become more salsa than ketchup.[1] More paella than pie. More tapas than toad-in-the-hole. A vulture for the local culture, you could say.

But when Covid-19 came along and coughed all over our livelihoods just six months into married life, we had no other option than to return home and start from scratch.

On Tenerife, aka the Island of Eternal Spring, we were living the sun-dappled pipe dream of so many. When we weren't on stage at night, most days our most difficult decision was having to choose which beach to visit with our camper van.

So, coming back from our dream life in the sun to the bleak northern weather, jobless, homeless and absolutely clueless about how to rebuild our lives, was a tough pill to swallow, especially when this was the time we'd planned to be starting a family. Instead we're starting from scratch.

Having the unfaltering support of my wife's parents who've agreed to put us up while we house hunt and job hunt has cushioned the crash back down to earth. As have all these friendly greetings that keep coming my way. Incredibly, a man over the road has actually just stopped, dropped the Home Bargains bags burdening both his arms to the floor and started waving at me.

Do I know him? I ask myself. I definitely don't. Well! These locals just get lovelier with every passing minute. I drop my guard, stop

---

1. This sentence was inspired by *More Ketchup Than Salsa*, a rib-tickling book written by a mate of mine, Joe Cawley.

worrying about "the others" coming back to "see me again", then smile and wave back. He responds by waving even more enthusiastically than before. His hand is going like a propeller. It feels a bit weird. A trifle forced. A tad unnatural, especially when the cars splashing through puddles in both directions temporarily make us lose sight of each other, but nonetheless, I still do the same. I don't know when to stop waving, so, not wanting to be rude, I'll stop when he stops, I deliberate.

Just when I suspect Propeller-Hands is about to take off, he finally gives his palm a rest and picks up his carrier bags. I retract my hand slowly, just in case he starts up again. He doesn't. I take a seat at one of the outside tables to tie a shoelace before walking off back into the rain. While doing so, I clock him crossing the road towards me. Surely he's not coming to talk to me as well? This makes me very nervous, but I don't want to be bad-mannered, so I stand up to greet him. As I get to my feet, he walks straight past me, goes into the café and joins a couple sat at a table by the window behind me.

I feel like an arse and hope nobody noticed. An old lady smoking to my left two tables away definitely did.

I think I'll draw the line at hello from now on.

Chapter 2

Getting Butter All the Time

18,304 of the buggers. That's how many the average Brit is believed to get through over the course of a lifetime.

Whatever could I be referring to? Rainy days? Hangovers? Cups of tea? Number of times a northerner scares a southerner by saying hello?

Good guesses, but no – sarnies! Sangers! Sandos! Sandwiches! That's what I'm talking about. Or, as I'm about to be reminded they call them up north, butties! And that's just what I need after a big swimming session to de-stress from a week of house hunting and job hunting – food. Bread. A BIG sandwich. Maybe even two of 'em!

A security alarm sounds a two-tone beep as I push open the door of a café across the road from the swimming baths. The eatery is a well-lit modern establishment that has all the shine and sheen of an IKEA showroom – laminate flooring; tall, wrought-iron black stalls tucked underneath chest-high, white-oak tables; mood spotlighting; the specials handwritten in yellow on a black chalkboard mounted on bright-white walls where framed photos of local celebrities have been proudly hung. There's Guy Garvey, lead singer of the indie rock band, Elbow; former Manchester United and England footballer, Gary Neville; the late, great actor and comedian, Victoria Wood. They're all stood next to the same proud-looking couple, who I assume to be the owners.

It seems I've chosen well. Locals eat here. And famous ones at that, from this very same town (I'll stop typing and let you Google where I am . . . Please be quick, though; I've just swum a mile and am very hungry!).

The tantalising smell of coffee percolating dances under my nose while I wait patiently to be served at the counter. As "Wonderwall" by Oasis plays through a tiny Bluetooth speaker atop the till, I eye up what's on offer in a glass display cabinet containing a variety of sandwich fillings: egg mayonnaise, meatballs, lamb chunks in marmalade. Okay, I admit that last one isn't true, but it wouldn't have surprised me given the ensuing madness.

The lady with bobbed brown hair from the photos on the wall eventually emerges through the bead curtains leading to a back room.

'What can I get you, loov?' she asks, slipping a pen into the top pocket of her white overalls.

'Chicken tikka sandwich on wholemeal bread, please.'

'Do you mean a butty?' she asks, her face contorting in confusion.

'Sorry. A, erm, yeah, a . . . butty, please,' I tentatively agree, not entirely sure if it does indeed mean the same thing as a sandwich. I've only ever heard of chip butties. 'You're not going to put chips in it, are you?' I double-check.

'No. Chicken tikka's not got chips in it, loov.'

I feel stupid. I put my hands in my pockets and look at the floor. Of course it bloody hasn't.

'I'll go see if we've got any bread left,' she says, then disappears from where she came out back through the bead curtains.

With the heating in the café cranked up, I take off my West Ham hat and move my messy, shoulder-length hair – which I still haven't got around to cutting thanks to lockdown – out of my eyes.

'I've not got that problem,' says a voice from behind me.

Turning around, I see a man I crossed paths with earlier in the swimming baths. He's now sat rustling a newspaper that I opine is only useful for rolling up the pages and stuffing inside wet shoes to dry them.

'Them were days,' he says, patting his big, shiny bald head that reflects the spotlighting. 'Don't 'aff pay get it cut anymore though!'

'Haha!' I say, pointing at him like he's a comedy genius.

I'd already haha'd him once today when we had a similarly strange exchange in the swimming bath changing rooms. I was drying myself when he came out the showers with a towel around his waist, trunks in hand.

'I must've been goin' fast,' he said, proudly poking two fingers through a hole in the crotch of his swimwear. 'Burnt a bloomin' hole in me trunks.'

While I do my best to think of something else to add to "haha" so he doesn't think that's all I'm capable of contributing to a conversation, two more hungry hippos enter the café. A youngish couple.

'What you had t'eat, Barr-eh?' the female in the couple asks the bald man.

'Lasagne. Bloomin' lovely,' Barry enthuses, patting his belly.

'You better not 'ad lot. That's what we're goin' 'aving.'

The lady serving me comes back to the counter.

'We've got no more bread in. White or brown. Sorr-eh.'

'No worries,' I say. 'Can I have it in a roll instead then, please?'

'A what?'

'A roll. One of those,' I say, pointing at a basket to her right.

'Do you mean a barm?'

'A what?'

'A baaaarm,' she repeats and presents me with what I recognise as a bread roll smeared in butter. Two decades of eating lunch down south has taught me as much.

'Barm, roll, whatever you call 'em. One of those'll do,' I accept. 'But can I have mine with no butter, please?'

'They've all got butter in,' she replies, looking at me like I've just asked if she can put some Covid-19 in it.

A male with a dark, shaggy mop top pops his head through the bead curtains leading out back and looks me up and down. Barry lowers the Daily Fail from his eyes. The couple waiting behind me stops talking. A fly on the wall stops buzzing. Cars outside skid to a halt. Gary Neville's jaw drops in the photo on the wall. Silence.

I reckon I might be the only customer they've ever had that has had the audacity to ask for no butter in their barmy roll.

I now feel under pressure to back down. To just say, 'You know what? Put butter everywhere. Spoon it into my coffee. Lubricate Barry's trunks with it so he stops burning holes in them. Stick it up Gary Neville's nose in the picture on the wall.' But curiosity gets the better of me. I just have to ask . . .

'They've ALL got butter in?'

'Yep,' she answers, 'take it or leave it.'

This never ever happened to me down south. I always had a choice. Butter, no butter or I Can't Believe It's Not Butter! But butter in every single barmy, rolly, breadular type-thing whether I liked it or not? This must be a northern quirk.

Feeling under duress to ingest butter against my wishes, I tell the younger couple to pass in front of me while I consider my options. They gratefully accept but take a wide berth as they step around me to place their order with the exasperated lady.

While they do, my eyes soon zero in on a basket full of bigger barms over the lady's shoulder. My stomach is rumbling with hunger pangs and my turn can't come back around quick enough. The lady doesn't look happy I'm still here when it does.

'Chicken tikka in one of those big barms, just there, please,' I say, pointing at them.

'You mean an oven bottom?'

'Eh?'

'They're called oven bottoms, not barms,' she says with ill-concealed irritation. I notice she's stopped calling me "loov".

'An oven bottom it is,' I concede, trying to bring the matter to a close without bloodshed.

'Do you want butter on it?' she asks, wielding a shiny knife that I hope is going to be used for buttering, not butchery.

'Aren't they all buttered?'

'Not the oven bottoms.'

'No butter then, thanks.'

We did it! And finally, bereft of butter!

The lady proceeds to stuff chicken tikka into my bottom as requested. While she does, her mop-topped male colleague comes out front to attend. He's quite clearly here for backup.

'What do you want to drink, pal?' he asks, rolling up his sleeves and rubbing his hands together like he's ready for a challenge. I know this is the point when I should back down. When I should de-escalate and conform. When I should ask for a cup of tea and milk with two butters. But I decide to push my luck and lay down one last challenge. One that risks me getting thrown out or the police being called.

'Can I have a latte, please?' I go gentle with him at first, then hit him with it: 'With almond milk.'

'Almond milk?!' Barry shouts from over my shoulder. 'You don't get teats on an almond!' he laughs, throwing down his paper on the table in amusement.

'No chance, pal,' says the man behind the counter.

'Normal milk'll do.'

'You're not from reauwnd 'ere, are you?' he asks over his shoulder while firing up the coffee machine.

'Essex boy,' I say.

'Explains a lot,' Barry jokes.

At long last, I sit down to eat alone at a table on the street outside. With a sense that Barry, the young couple and the owners are inside talking about me and watching my every move, I bury my face in my bottom, chewing on a very positive thought – it's good to know where my bread is buttered so far from home.

Chapter 3

Rasher Decision

"Argh! They're about as useful as a hairbrush in a bloody hurricane!" I raged to Rachel, who was in tears at hearing the news that our flights back to the UK from Tenerife had been cancelled for a third, frustrating time.

In hindsight, I accept the British Government was probably right to restrict international arrivals during the peak of second wave infections, but my fuse blew in the heat of the moment.

At that point we'd been living off our dwindling savings for nearly five months because our careers had been criminalised and we couldn't go to work. Those elusive flights home to a fresh start were the faintest of lights at the end of a tunnel that just seemed to be getting darker and longer.

Lockdown had turned our lives upside down from day one. First, we had to deal with the financial stress that we'd have no work or money coming in until further notice. Two weeks into lockdown, a close friend of ours tragically died of a heart attack. Just a week later, my 87-year-old nan was taken by bowel cancer. It was truly heartbreaking that we were unable to pay our respects to either of them in the traditional way due to lockdown.

My normal way of dealing with such stress would be to go out and run until I could run no more. Since we weren't even allowed to leave the house to exercise during the first 50 days of the draconian Spanish lockdown, I had to find other ways to de-stress.

To keep a level head and a balanced sense of perspective during those trying times, I absorbed all the inspirational speeches, interviews and books I could lay my eyes and ears on. I had to seek out people talking sense while my mind was garbling negative nonsense.

I soon stumbled across the work of author and speaker, Mo Gawdat, and an approach he calls "committed acceptance." This, he says, "is accepting the harshness of life and the things we can't change, whilst at the same time committing to making tomorrow a little better than today."

Upon finally returning home on separate flights (another calamitous tale deserving of its own book), the most obvious way we could make things better was by securing any form of employment and a place to live.

A month after reuniting up north, we tick both off the list. I've secured a post teaching English remotely after completing an online qualification I started at the very beginning of lockdown, and Rachel has got a job in a primary school as a Teaching Assistant.

In another stroke of luck, we discover a friend of Rachel's friend has a house available to rent. We view our soon-to-be-new humble abode, agree on a very fair monthly fee, pump fists with the landlord because we can't handshake and are handed the keys. We also count our lucky stars that we were allowed to move in when the vast majority of landlords wouldn't even let us view their properties because we came with a pet in tow – our rescue dog, Pearl.

When it came to naming the little black bag of bones who was found starving and dying with fur in dreadlocks in the Tenerife mountains, we drew inspiration from our musical muses. Since Rachel's favourite artist is Lionel Richie and mine is Pearl Jam, the latter was deemed more fitting for a female dog. We both settled on Pearl, with Rachel bargaining that our first child, if we're lucky enough to have one, will be called Lionel if it's got a dinky. I kept my mouth shut that I intend to name it Leaf, boy or girl.

Our rental payments are twice the price of our Spanish mortgage, and our new jobs pay a sobering amount less per hour than we were earning pre-Covid, but we're just about covering our costs again.

For the first time in a turbulent and traumatic six months, we're on relatively stable ground where we can find our feet and rebuild our lives.

This can mean only one thing after such a stinking shit of a show – we must celebrate! In Tenerife we'd have slipped on our flip flops, shades and beach wear, then gone for a sun, surf and tapas day out in our camper van. But now, we're in Bolton. So, on a rainy Sunday morning, we put on our waterproofs and climb aboard the 471 Bolton to Bury bus and go for a sandwich. I mean butty.

After nearly getting barred from the last place where I asked for a sandwich, my confidence in my ability to order refreshments is a little fragile. The only other occasion I remember being so confused placing an order was when I did so at a beach hut in Brazil. I bought a coffee from a man who, to my shock and surprise, turned out to be stark, bollock naked. Unbeknown to me, I'd strayed to a nudist beach. With coffee in hand, I hurried away as his testicles swung like two brussels sprouts in a mouse's sleeping bag. I declined his offer of sugar just in case he used his impressive stirrer.

As uncomfortable as that moment was, at least I had an answer and could pull it off (ordering the coffee, I mean). I knew what to say and do to get out of there before he could ask me if I've got a reward card he'd stamp with his Brazil nuts.

Once again, just a week after getting butter all the time in the café just across the road from where I am now, I'm served up yet another culinary curveball.

With Rachel, I enter Wax and Beans, a trendy establishment that doubles up as a vinyl-selling coffee shop. She goes to save us the only free table and I have to queue for quite some time at the counter behind a man that's requested the record *What's Going On* by Marvin Gaye.

'Has to be the Original Detroit Mix,' the keen vinyl collector specifies with a cautionary finger.

Nothing is too much trouble for a very approachable, bubbly and smiley silver fox of a man behind the counter who's wiggling a mouse around (on a computer, not a real, live one. That wouldn't be good for custom) scanning their back catalogue for the requested "33-inch."

'Your luck's in,' says the silver fox. 'We have one pre-loved, stunning, imported Japanese edition.'

'I'll take it!' The customer smiles gratefully, digging out his wallet from his trouser pocket.

'So, that's 5,499 English pennies, please,' says the silver fox in the politest of tones.

'Eh?! Five grand?!' chokes the customer.

'Of pennies, yeah,' confirms the silver fox who has all the brightness and bubbliness of a children's TV presenter. '£54.99! Just for you, sir.'

'Bloomin 'eck! I were about to tell you to stick it!' says the customer, visibly relieved.

While I'm standing in the queue waiting patiently as vinyl and legal tender changes hands, a waitress comes out the kitchen carrying in one hand a mug and in the other a sizzling bacon sandwich. On a plate, of course, not actually in her hand. That'd be messy business, unhygienic and would probably get the place closed down.

That unmistakable, enticing and entrancing smell of cooked bacon ignites my appetite. I'll have some of that, I think to myself.

My turn to order finally arrives when the man in front of me walks slowly out of the shop, examining his Marvin Gaye record with a forensic level of attention to make sure it's the exact edition for which he's parted with thousands of pennies.

'Two cappuccinos, please,' I ask the young waitress wearing an autumn-brown apron who was just carrying the bacon sandwich.

'Want sugar with that?' she checks, re-tying her pony-tailed, bleach-blond hair.

'One with, one without, please. Also, can I get a cheese toastie for my wife sat over there?' I say, pointing to Rachel who's sat by the window championing vegetarianism and kindness to animals in her grey "I don't eat anything that poops" jumper.

'And a bacon sandwich – sorry, I mean a butty – a bacon butty for me, please?'

'Oooooh-keeeeh . . .' she says, tapping away at a tactile screen. While she does, I remember what the Barry White lady said on the bus about cheese toasties. I tell myself I must not think about her sticky front bum when I see Rachel bite into her sandwich.

'Ow'd you like your bacon?' the waitress checks, interrupting those unsettling thoughts.

This is the moment when things get complicated. When I falter and the colour drains from my face. Never have I ever been asked, whether it be on my travels, during my years in Spain or growing up down south, how I like my bacon. Every single time, the keeper of the bacon just slipped it in there. No special requests were necessary. No further questions asked. Which is why, I confess, I don't know how

I like my pig. Do you? If you do, tell me, what do I say here? In a blanket? Flying? Smoky, like the crisps? I mean, I know how I like my eggs (of the Scotch kind); my saveloy (preceded by an "oi oi!"); my pies (with mash and jellied eels like most folk with East London blood like myself). But my bacon? Nope. I've got nothing.

Adam pokes his head out of my neck, then takes a bite out of his apple to see how I'll handle this.

'What are the options?' I whisper back to the girl with a panicked look in my eyes that says, "Why would you do this to me in front of all these people?"

'Erm . . . crisp-eh?' she suggests.

'That'll do. Crispy,' I quickly accept, sweating into my Covid mask.

I was going to ask for no butter. I dare not now. I can't take any more humiliation.

'Just so you know for next time, it's table service only because of Covid.' She politely yet sternly wrist-slaps me. 'You only queue up if you want to ask about a record.'

'Oh. Sorry,' I apologise, wondering why she didn't tell me that in the first place.

Before I walk over to where Rachel is sat at a table by the window, I surreptitiously scan the room to see if anyone else has seen the very public shame of my poor bacon game. Patrons, young and old, are lost in quiet, muffled conversation. Sole diners are thumbing messages into their phones. Vinyl enthusiasts are sifting through record racks on the walls. Cutlery is clanging on crockery. Mobiles are pinging, dinging and ringing notifications.

The smell of my fear is still present, too. A man comes out the toilet shaking his wet fingers with the dryer still droning. As he walks past, giving off a whiff of hand sanitiser, I wonder if he's just washed his hands of me after hearing about my inability to make a rasher decision.

American folk rocker Ryan Adams is playing quietly through the house speakers in the background. 'And everybody knoooooows. Everybody knows,' he wails. The lyrics make me even more paranoid.

I tiptoe across the creaky wooden floorboards, checking through the window to see if the barmy, butty lady with the big bottoms from across the road has caught wind and is coming over to throw some butter at me for me being such an awkward customer again. Thankfully, she hasn't and isn't.

I'm relieved that no one, aside from the waitress, knows. My bacon has been saved, it would seem.

I pull out a seat praying to God Rachel hasn't chosen the wobbly table. I can't handle a wobbly table and bacongate all in the same day. It does wobble a little, but not as much as I did when asked how I like my bacon. As I plant my bum on the chair, Rachel is indulging in her single biggest obsession – taking photos. She has more than 16,000 pictures on her smartphone. She'll take pictures of anything and everything. Even toilets, if she thinks they're nice.

'I just want to remember every moment,' she endearingly replied when I first asked why she thought such random, seemingly meaningless paraphernalia were worthy of precious storage space on her phone.

As I remove my Covid mask, she's capturing the upholstery cover on one of the spare chairs at our table.

'What's *Dark Side of the Moon*?' she asks.

'It's a Pink Floyd album,' I fill her in.

'What about that one?' she asks again, pointing at the other empty chair at our table.

'*Definitely Maybe* by Oasis. The chair covers are all iconic rock album covers,' I say.

'I'm a Motown kinda gal.' Rachel shrugs. 'I'd never know.'

'How come you look like the cat that's got the cream?' I ask, changing the subject.

'Well, now we've got some money coming in again,' she says brightly, snapping her laptop closed, 'I've just ordered a stack of cards from Card Factory's website – 26p each!' she chirps, ticking off a long list of upcoming birthdays in her diary.

'This is why I love you, baby,' I say. 'Always thinking of others.'

'And, why did I buy these?' she tests me, reopening her laptop and spinning it around to display pictures of a magnifying glass and a fake smoking pipe.

'I don't know, why did you buy them?'

'Come on. Think,' she says. 'What series are we watching?'

'Erm,' I rack my brains. '*Elementary!*'

'And, who are the main characters?' she asks.

'Sherlock Holmes and Watson.'

'That's who we're dressing up as when we start the next season,' she says, her face suffused with enthusiasm.

I should've known. When the latest season of the American sitcom *Big Bang Theory* dropped, Rachel bought us frumpy clothes to dress up as two of the protagonists, Amy and Sheldon. When we went to see the last *Bond* film, she made me wear a tuxedo and go as James while she dressed up as Miss Moneypenny. You get the picture by now, I'm sure. Rachel's a bit, what's the word? Extra. But she's a delight, too! And I wouldn't want her any other way.

When our butties arrive, Rachel takes a photo of her cheese toasty and coffee while I look my crispy bacon butty up and down. This better be bloody good after all this stress, I think to myself. I take a bite. I chew. I chew a bit faster. My palate purrs. I swallow. My stomach aches for more. It's better than good. It's a tastegasm!

'Take a photo of my sandwich as well,' I beg Rachel. 'This is a moment I want to remember.'

Who needs sun, surf and tapas or pie and mash when you've got crispy bacon buttwiches?

Chapter 4

Saucy Sauce

"Are English people honest and direct?"

I found this query posted on Quora, a question-and-answer-based website with over 300 million users per month.

From the countless replies, this post by a certain Thurza Jones caught my eye:

> **"While southerners will smile at you while plotting to kill you, northerners are more honest, direct and straight to the point."**

How can we argue with Thurza Jones, an author who is a respected voice of authority on Quora with more than 1.7 million answer views and, like me, can talk from experience as a southerner living in the north?

These signature traits to which Thurza refers are no more evident than in the tell-it-like-it-is christening of some of the north's most famous culinary creations: Sticky Toffee Pudding (Cartmel, Cumbria – official date disputed); Mushy Peas (rumour has it Manchester area, mid-1800s); Yorkshire Pudding (estimated early 1700s).

Thankfully, this literal approach was not adopted when naming the southern dessert, Dorset Knob. Imagine that turning up on your plate with a spotted dick?

One late October evening, I happen across another culinary themed example of northerners telling it like it is . . .

Friday, 6 p.m., skies already charcoal, we pull up outside Rachel's grandad's house. A wind-powered beer can is noisily racing a squadron of crispy fallen leaves down the road as we walk up his driveway and press the doorbell. Through the frosted glass of the front door we hear the flick of light switches, then see a shadow advance to the tune of "We Wish You a Merry Christmas." Her grandad, Stanley, loves the season to be jolly so much that he insists on having it as his permanent, year-round doorbell.

'Waheeeey!' he cries in surprise upon opening his front door.

'Don't come near me, Grandad,' Rachel warns as he comes to her for a hug. 'I'm in school every day with hundreds of sneezing and coughing kids.'

'Oh bloomin' 'eck, not you as well!' he tuts before quickly getting over it and moving onto more important matters. ''Ere! Never guess what . . . they just said on't telly – two minutes and 39 seconds f'choco-late bourbon!' he explains, eyes popping in amazement. 'Bloomin' biscuit dippin' world record!'

Stanley Lee loves tea and just can't get enough of the stuff. The first time we met on a family holiday in Tenerife, I offered him a themed hat to put on during a night out at a Mexican restaurant.

'Would you like to wear a sombrero, Stanley?' I suggested.

'I'll 'ave a cuppa tea,' came his answer.

While the family swilled chilled margaritas in merriment in sub-tropical climes, Stanley nursed cup after steaming cup of his beloved brew, sombrero on his bonce.

Once Stanley gets chatting about tea, there's often no stopping him, even while outside his front door with the rain starting to dampen our clothes.

'T'other week, doctor said overt' phone, nine sugars in me tea were too much,' he complains, wiping rain off his glasses with the sleeve of his Bolton Wanderers jumper.

'Me dad used 'ave nine sugars and he lived 'til he were ninety-bloomin'-two! I'm only 'aving two now,' he sighs. 'I said t'doctor, if I don't live 'til I'm 92, it's all your bloomin' fault.'

The charity, Age UK, estimates that there are 1.4 million chronically lonely older people in England. Even more heart-wrenching, in 2015, the Office for National Statistics concluded that loneliness is correlated to an increased mortality risk of 26%.

Rachel's family have been doing all they can throughout lockdown to make sure Stanley doesn't become another tragic statistic. As well as his grandchildren and children taking turns to coordinate Sunday afternoon doorstep visits, Rachel's mum and dad have kept up a tradition they've maintained for many years: Fish Friday.

Every Friday evening after work, come rain or shine, they've taken him for fish and chips at his local Wetherspoons pub. With that not being possible due to the suspected bat bug flying around, they've taken to doorstep deliveries instead to keep the custom alive.

Despite her family's team efforts to maintain that life-saving family contact, Rachel is still worried her grandad is feeling lonely when she gets a notification that he was playing basketball at 2am.

To give him a nice surprise and lift his spirits, she suggested we do the honours of delivering his Fish Friday instead of her parents.

Stanley was, by the way, playing a basketball simulation on Facebook, not the real game of course. Although he's an 80-something who worked as a block paver until he was 79, knows how to use a smart phone, still drives and walks his dog twice per day, the only thing you're likely to catch him dunking is a biscuit in his tea.

'Ready for your chippy tea, Grandad, before it gets cold?' Rachel asks, prompting him to move inside where it's warmer.

'Your mum and dad not coming?' he asks.

'Not tonight. Me and Brad wanted to have Fish Friday with you this week, give you a nice surprise,' she says, passing him the takeaway carrier bags.

'Ooooh thank you. Smells bloomin' lovely!' he enthuses, sniffing at the bags. 'They're not garden peas, are they?' He peers suspiciously into the bags. 'Last time they were hard as bugger and I were chasing 'em round plate.'

'Mushy, Grandad,' Rachel confirms. 'Just the way you like 'em.'

As part of Stanley's Fish Friday special, Rachel has suggested we have "tea" together (my fellow southerners, please note that's a northerner's evening meal, not a beverage). Though we can't do it together in his house without risking a ten-grand fine, we can do it on FaceTime from our homes.

'See you soon on your phone, Stanley,' I shout out the car window as Rachel reverses off his drive.

Leaning out of his front door with childlike excitement in his 84-year-old blue eyes, he waves us off until we turn the corner to the next street and are out of sight.

On the drive back home, as Rachel sings at the top of her voice to Lionel Richie on her favourite station, Smooth FM, it dawns on me that's exactly what our life abroad was missing – loved ones that wave you off until you're out of sight. I well up thinking about just how special that wave was and how such simple gestures can mean so much, lift one's spirits and bring warmth and sunshine into our lives even on the coldest of nights.

Twenty minutes later, we're back home sat at our dining room table, FaceTiming her grandad in his living room.

''Ow's yer chips, Grandad?' Rachel asks, leaning her phone against a ketchup bottle to keep it stable.

'Me what?' he shouts back, adjusting his hearing aid so he can hear Rachel on his phone.

'Yer cod. And yer chips. How's your cod and chips?'

'Me hips?' he says, looking down and tapping his hips with both hands. 'Yeah, alright . . .'

'Not your hips. Your chips.' Rachel dangles a soggy chip in front of the camera. 'And your fish,' she says before using a hand to exaggerate a big fish swimming in the sea.

'Bloomin' lovely. Thanks again for bring-gin' 'em.'

'Turn your telly down,' Rachel says, 'you might be able 'ear me better.'

Taking Rachel's suggestion on board, he grabs the remote, lowers the volume, then throws it onto the sofa behind him.

Despite the TV being silenced, the conversation carries on in this vein with Rachel having to repeat most of what she says several times to be understood.

'You having your usual – custard, for your pudding?' Rachel asks as she snaps a screenshot of their smiling faces on her phone.

'Hot dog? Am I 'avin' hot dog?' Stanley replies.

'Not hot dog. Custard. For your pudding,' Rachel mouths back, pretending to spoon custard out of a bowl.

I munch away on my fish and chips at the table next to Rachel, thinking that she really does have the patience of a saint and a heart as big as the hole in the crotch of Barry's swimming trunks.

Once we've finished off our takeaways and Rachel's all but lost her voice from shouting her way through the FaceTime dinner date, Stanley insists on giving us a grand tour of his recently revamped living room.

Just like always, there's pictures of his seven grandkids at different ages bedecking the walls; a floral shrine around a framed photo and the urn of his late wife, Stella, on the mantelpiece; his golden retriever, Millie, snoozing at the foot of Stanley's armchair. He's also made a few new installations that he presents like a bikini-clad gameshow assistant: a giant poster of Bolton Wanderers' fixture list has been blue-tacked to the living room door; a brand new leather sofa replete with Bluetooth speaker has replaced his old one and a snooker tabletop has been slid onto the living room dining table.

'I've been playing snooker on me own,' he says, simulating a shot with an air cue.

'You've not?' Rachels says, her heart breaking for him.

'I 'ave. I'm getting good again.'

'Soon as we can, we'll come over and give you a game,' Rachel promises.

'I hope so. I love it. I just love it when you come see me,' he gushes. 'Eh! Look at this.' He takes a seat on his new sofa. Lifting up one of the arms, he activates the Bluetooth, then presses "play" on his phone. Seconds later, we're listening to the sofa booming out "Money, Money, Money" by ABBA. Stepping in time to the beat, he picks up a cushion emblazoned with a photo of all the grandkids together, holds it up to the screen, and gives it a hug. Rather randomly, memories come flooding back of the day my own late grandfather, Johnny Smith, proudly showed us his colostomy bag languishing on his pallid stomach.

'Works like a treat, this,' my grandad said, lifting up his jumper and patting his colostomy bag affectionately like a pet.

I've not been able to eat a boil-in-the-bag curry since.

As Stanley endearingly dances to ABBA, hugging the pillow of his grandkids, I notice there's a woman on Stanley's television. It's not just any woman. It's a woman who seems to be a little absent minded because she's forgotten to get dressed before going on air. She appears to be very lonely in lockdown too, because she's shaking a phone in her hand, begging people to call her. I give Rachel a nudge in the ribs to make her aware that he's got Babestation on in the background.

'Who's that on ya telly, Grandad?' Rachel shouts over ABBA.

'You what?' he says, turning off the music.

'You've got some lady on your telly, look!' Rachel says, pointing at the female shaking her surgically enhanced chesticles on the TV screen over his shoulder.

'That's not *Antiques Roadshow* what I were watching before!' Stanley says in confusion. 'She 'as got nice cups, though!' he laughs.

'Grandad!' Rachels tells him off. 'It must've changed channel when you threw the remote on the sofa,' she says, trying to play it down and not get involved in a conversation about a glamour model's cups.

'Eh! Your nan 'ad some right belters just like she's got on,' he says, pointing at the woman who's now showing off her undercarriage.

'I've still got your nan's naughties in a box upstairs. We used 'ave some right saucy sauce.'

Saucy sauce. Honest, direct and straight to the point. Thurza, you may rest your case.

Chapter 5

Bunion Beryl

'I 've got bunions y'see, so I 'aff wear me driving shoes instead of me cowgirl boots for line dancing.'

Meet Beryl, everyone. I bumped into this lovely lady with wispy, shoulder-length grey hair in the woods literally seconds ago at dusk. She's about to teach me that not only do the locals like to say hello, they also love to stop, chat and talk about their ailments. Well, Beryl (whose real name I've changed so she doesn't feel silly if she ever reads this) certainly does, anyway.

'Me friend Shirley said to put hairdryer on me bunion. Stretches skin out, she said. I were there bloomin' hours, I were,' she complains. 'Didn't bloomin' work. Just made me foot hot.'

'And these,' Beryl says, lifting a muddy walking boot. 'Forty pound, they were, int' sale. Me granddaughter, she says they're all the range!'

Doesn't she mean rage, as in, all the rage? I think to myself as my phone interrupts Beryl's footnotes with a loud burp. Yes, I'm well aware I should probably have a more grown-up notification tone for my messages, but I downloaded it because it makes me giggle every time it goes off. And, since laughing has been proven to boost our immune systems, release stress and help us live seven years longer on average, I'm keeping it. And no, I'm not childish. You're childish. Talk about yourself, why don't you, you poohead.

'That was my phone burping by the way, not me,' I plead my innocence, presenting it from my coat pocket.

'All things must pass,' Beryl says, poo-pooing my penchant for noisy bodily functions.

Before I can read the first message, my phone burps another. It's Rachel.

> *Roast's nearly ready baby. Half hour more in the oven x.*

Time is now of the essence. If I'm not home in 30 minutes, Rachel will kill me because this is not just any Sunday roast. It's a Sunday roast at which my wife wants to commemorate three years to the day since we met Roy Walker. She's even gone out and bought the board game Catchphrase for us to play after dinner so I MUST NOT be late.

We met when the former host of the popular TV game show was a VIP guest at a dinner and dance affair, Showtime Live, in which Rachel and I were once both cast members.

'Was your chicken okay, Roy?' was the best conversation starter Rachel could hatch when the cast were introduced to him post-show.

'Aye, hit the spot,' Roy replied before smiling warmly for a photo with us. He was a true gent.

Back to the present, I must pluck up the courage to cut the conversation with Beryl short as soon as possible without being rude and ruffling her feathers (the chicken puns are now over – promise!). Make no bones about it (I lied), not only are many husband brownie points at stake if I'm late for Rachel's Roy Walker Roast, but so is our safety. Beryl and I must escape from these daunting and darkening woods before the weed-smoking, electric scooter crew comes rolling out of the shadows in their hoodies with their blinding lights at sundown and the squirrels turn nasty in their hunt for nuts.

My spine freezes with fear when I realise I have a precious two of my own at risk. Right on cue, a crow lurking somewhere high amongst the tree tops caws a haunting call. As I put my hands in my pockets to protect my crown jewels, Beryl, in ignorant bliss to the clear and present danger, carries on giving me the lowdown on her feet and footwear.

'Before'wa, I were using sandals int' summer. But I've got corns too now, y'see,' she says, pointing at her right foot.

It reminds me of how Rachel likes to add sweetcorn to her roast dinners. I'll struggle to eat it now that Beryl has put a corny right foot in my appetite.

A squirrel skitters up a muddy steep bank behind us through the brittle fallen leaves. Hopefully Beryl's put him off his nuts (and mine) with all this feet fungi talk.

Another problem has arisen, further complicating matters: her Irish terrier, Dennis. He seemed harmless at first when I stopped to stroke him, but now he's pulling on his lead and trying to plunge his snout between my dog Pearl's back legs and into her fur burger. This is all Dennis' fault. If he hadn't jumped up at me as we passed on the paved path snaking through the woods, Beryl wouldn't have trapped me in this one-way conversation.

Dennis' body is now shaking and he's making groaning and grunting "give me your puppies, bitch!" noises. Pearl, half Dennis' size, has taken evasive action and is now cowering and whining behind me.

'He's always like this,' Beryl says. 'Even wit' bloomin' rockweilers.'

Doesn't she mean rottweilers? I ponder as she points at Pearl.

'It's like he's gonna eat your dog alive like Animal Lecter.'

And here's me all this time thinking that lecherous character from *The Silence of the Lambs* film was called Hannibal Lecter, not Animal Lecter. Maybe the world isn't round after all?

'Takes the bloody picnic sometimes, he does,' she says, clapping a hand to her forehead with an exasperated sigh.

Hang on. It's take the biscuit, isn't it? Surely? Am I going mad?

'What's this pretty little thing called?' Beryl asks, bringing me back from the land of confusion.

'Pearl,' I say, patting her on the head.

'What breed is she?'

'She's a rescue dog so we'll never know for sure, but we reckon she's a cross between a spaniel and a collie. We call her a spollie.'

'Awww, bless, she looks like a little puppy,' Beryl says, stroking Pearl's head.

'The vets think she's about seven years old,' I say. 'Well,' I declare, seizing on the first lull in the conversation so I can get home in time for Rachel's roast. 'Really nice to –'

'What were amazin',' she cuts in, not sensing my restlessness to get going, 'them summer sandals I bought were size five, y'see. But I'm size five n' half. Fitted like a glove, they did,' she says, slipping her right hand into an imaginary glove. 'I couldn't believe me luck.'

The smell of burning log fires emanates from a row of terraced houses looking down on the woods to our right. Lights in the bedrooms are beginning to flicker on. A siren wails from a revving police car as it drops down a gear to speed up on a nearby road. A squirrel turns on their headlamp and sharpens their claws in preparation for Operation Night Nuts. Time to get out of these woods with both of mine is running out.

'I've got a fake knee too, y'see,' she says, tapping her left knee. 'Don't bloomin' stop me though. Even at 71!'

I wish you would stop, please! I have to be home in 26 minutes, rain is starting to drum ever faster and heavier in the stream running alongside us, and I can now smell marijuana which can mean only one thing – the electric scooter hoodie crew is advancing!

Dennis is undeterred and now out of control. He's humping mid-air and has started barking, too. Piercingly loud. Pearl's whining escalates a couple of pitches as I wave a stick in front of Dennis' nose to sidetrack him. It doesn't work. He's more interested in his own stick. His red lipstick that he's jousting in Pearl's direction. His weapon of mass reproduction. Looks like Pigs in Blankets. I'll have to pass on those now, too.

'I just love doin' up me house, y'see. Me hubby tries tell me give it a rest fetching new furniture. I tell him he's off his rocket if he thinks he's going stopping me!'

Surely she means rocker? Off his rocker?

'He won't do up house anymore, y'see. He's got arthritis int' spine.'

'Sorry to hear th –'

'It's a shame, because he's got 50/50 vision and a very good eye f'detail.'

'Fifty-fifty vision?' I check.

'That's right.'

I wonder what 20/20 vision is, then.

'Me son, he's got rheumatoid arthritis. Lives in moor-waz y'see, near Burnley,' she says, waving over the top of the dripping trees ahead of us to where the moors just might be.

'When he got flooded, it were me that shoved all sofas and chairs out'ta way. I try not moddycoddle him but it's hard not to, int'it?'

Moddycoddle? Doesn't she mean "mollycoddle"?

I put my hood up and shiver as ice rain drips down the back of my neck from the bare branches overhead.

'You're not from reauwnd here, are you?' she says out of nowhere, pointing in my face. 'Yoooou've got a cockney accent!'

This takes me by surprise for many reasons. One, because I was discreetly checking the time. Two, because she says it like it's an accusation. And three, because I got the impression she hasn't really been listening to me.

'I'm from up road, y'see,' she goes on. 'Sixty-one years I've lived ont' Park Street.'

Shit! She lives on the same street as me. What if she comes round and asks me to hairdryer her bunion and bite off her corns?

'Where'd you live?' she asks.

'Over there,' I signal in a very general direction back over my shoulder.

'What street's that?'

Don't tell her. Whatever you do, don't let it slip that you live on the same street.

'Um, errrr . . . I just moved up here. You know what? I can't even remember the name of the street!' I lie through my teeth and throw my arms open in a well-would-you-believe-it kind of way.

'I used'go Sunday school at church up there. Saint Franny's.'

Great! I've thrown her off the scent.

'An' 'im,' she says, pointing at Dennis who's still very much on Pearl's petrified scent, 'he's had heart murmurs. Vet gave him some tablets that made his toilet yellow.'

That's put me off the mustard for my roast.

'Not keeping you, am I? Me name's Beryl, by the way.'

This is it. My long and patiently awaited opportunity to cry for mercy and plead, 'We must end this, Beryl By The Way! The woods are getting darker with every second and we're going to get mowed down and mugged by the electric scooter crew! It's bloody baltic and raining and I can't feel my hands anymore and we're going to die of hypothermia! I'm going to be thinking of your foot corn, bunions and Dennis' dripping lipstick and his yellow toilet, if I'm ever able to get home to celebrate meeting Roy Walker. I can't take anymore! Please, Beryl By The Way! Please release me before Dennis the dirty dog docks at Pearl's puppy port.'

But I just can't. I just don't have the heart to stop her in full flow and tell her she's keeping me. To break it to her that I'm from down south where I've been socially reared to avoid this whole stop-and-chat-to-strangers thing, and that I'm out of my depth here. Beryl is full on. She's overbearing. She's got verbal diarrhoea and yaps more than a chihuahua on Red Bull and Skittles. She's the epitome of "small doses." But she's also very nice, harmless and dare I say it, loveable.

'Which way you going, Beryl?' I enquire, trying to get us moving at least.

'Over there, t'wards dentist.'

Fearing she's about to unleash her dental records, show me her fillings and present her dentures for inspection, I take the bit by the teeth.

'Shall we walk and talk?' I propose, even though she's going the opposite direction to my house.

'Go on then,' she says. 'Be dark soon and all the rum'uns[1] will be out.'

Progress!

---

1. A naughty or mischievous person. Down south they might be called an "oik", "scallywag" or a "toe rag".

As our footsteps reverberate across a wooden footbridge that tra-verses the stream carving through the woods, I thumb Rachel a mes-sage:

> *Running a little late. Walking an old lady home I met in the woods. Won't be long . . .*

Rachel soon burps back:

> *You're a good'un.*

Phew! No brownie points lost.

'So me son,' Beryl resumes, 'when his house got flooded and I were helping move his furniture, it were all squeaking. I said to him, you need some UB40 . . .'

Chapter 6

Trolley Dolly

Since we met four years ago, I've become quite the expert at decoding Rachel's repertoire of exclamations.

A sudden cry of 'Braaaaaaaad!' at a conversational pitch means she's been spooked by the presence of a life-threatening beast like an ant, beetle or ladybird.

A panicked shriek of 'Braaaaaaaad!' in an ear-drum-splitting pitch means that a spider, moth, daddy longlegs or some other winged or multi-limbed invader is holding her captive.

A guttural growl of 'Braaaaaaaad!' in her lowest, darkest, angriest tone invariably means I've done something very wrong and she's about to scratch my name into the bad books.

Of course, I knew nothing of these loveable quirks of her character the night we met at one of my gigs. When we were introduced by mutual acquaintances post-show and a quick chat turned into a few drinks and a kebab and a garlic sauce-flavoured snog in my camper van at sunrise, I was painfully honest and got straight to the point.

'You could definitely find a younger, more handsome man than me,' I acknowledged when I dropped her home as the sun came up.

'I'm a granny at heart,' Rachel pleaded, putting her hand on my hand resting on the gearstick (not my gearstick).

It was important for me to get the 13-year age gap out in the open before we started dating and make sure we both wanted the same things: settle down, get married, start a family, call the kids Leaf, Flame and Clive (I left out the bit about the names), then live happily ever after drinking out of novelty mugs (Rachel is addicted to them).

Rachel insisted she did want all those things, especially the novelty mugs. I'd soon find out she's obsessed with them and changes mugs depending on mood, occasions and seasons. As I type up this chapter, she's downstairs watching *The Great British Bake Off* whilst sipping coffee from her "Snuggle up, it's cold outside" autumn mug.

I often get told that Rachel is "out of my league." That "I'm punching." This is because I look like Jim Carrey while Rachel is a stunningly beautiful brunette with mermaid-length hair and the kindest and prettiest of smiles that melts my heart. Not only is she a stunner, inside and out, she's also a young lady with an old soul, yesteryear values and far more mature than I can ever hope to be. If I were to say she looked like someone famous, it would be her dad. He's famous down his local church hall where he volunteers his services every Saturday night as DJ Disco Dave the Rave.

If I'd known on the night we met that she squeezes the toothpaste from the top, talks over films and series so I have to watch them with subtitles, and mutates into a horn-hooting, road-raging, light-flashing Boltonian devil behind the wheel, I still would've wanted to be with her. I have far worse traits, as you're about to find out.

'Braaaaaaaad!' Rachel snarls from the kitchen in that gravely bad-book tone while I'm watching football in the living room.

Uh oh . . .

'You've eaten all the eggs!' Rachel summons me.

'Have I?' I reply, knowing full well that I have but not remembering the reason why this means I'm now a bad egg.

'Yes you have, you swine. I was saving them to bake Grandad's birthday cake.'

I feel bad. Very bad. Bad like the time when I flushed the chain on the toilet and made the shower turn cold and Rachel scream. This is far worse though, because I now recall being reminded earlier in the week not to eat those eggs so she could bake a cake for her grandad Stanley's 84th. But I've scrambled those plans by forgetting and devouring nine of them for my breakfasts throughout the week.

'You'll have to go get some,' Rachel hisses, arms crossed, brandishing a wooden spoon.

In touristy Tenerife, this wouldn't have been a problem with shops open round the clock to serve the demands of legless holidaymakers. But being eggless on a Sunday evening in residential England, when it's out of hours for the behemoth superstores during lockdown, presents a challenge. One to which I must rise so that the cake flour can, too.

I search for "*supermarkets nearby*" on my phone.

'There's a store called NISA two miles away,' I announce. 'I'll drive down there.'

Rachel replies with a stony silence and an angry, frustrated and haunting bang of a wooden spoon on a cake mix bowl. My head could quite easily be that bowl if I don't poach some eggs from somewhere, sometime soon.

Vowing to put this wrong oh-so right so that I don't have to walk on eggshells for the next week, I jump in the car before Rachel throws me in the doghouse. Little did I know the crazy corner of northwest England I was about to discover.

Five minutes later, after having thrown a few Lennies and Ronnies (as some of us southerners call left and right) I'm following the satnav down a long, dark street of red-bricked terraced houses, many of them with their doors and windows boarded up. One of them has a "keep out" warning in white graffiti on the red brickwork. Another has a broken fridge, door wide open on the front lawn-cum-jungle. It's like browsing wrongmove.com.

As I press the lock all doors button, I remember the time a letting agent showed me a 25-square-metre bedsit in a similarly scarred part of London when I'd just left university. She wanted a grand a month and spun the area as "sprinkled with up and coming character properties." Truth is, it was down, gone and never coming back, just like the street I'm driving down.

More than a decade later, our three bedroom house with garden, garage and two bathrooms costs us two-thirds of that price. A prime example of how much further your pound can stretch up north compared to down south.

Continuing down the road, up ahead on the left-hand side, my headlights pick out the place that's going to save the day – a dimly lit NISA supermarket occupying a commercial unit on the ground floor of a grubby high rise. Outside, there's a couple with cans in hands, having what appears to be an alcohol-fuelled argument under a strobing lamppost. The man wobbles like a baby taking its first ever steps and points an accusatory finger that misses his intended target. Off balance and probably out of focus, he's now picking a fight with the lamppost instead. Thankfully, the lamppost makes light of the situation and doesn't retaliate. The woman stumbles herself a little, then stomps off, throwing her arms around in a toddler-like tantrum. The same scene, minus the wobbling, stumbling, alcohol and strobe lighting, may well play out in my house if I don't score some eggs.

On the pavement to my right, three hooded boys around 10 years old on BMX bikes go racing past before pedalling off down a back street. I wonder what mischief they're out creating so long after dark.

When I creak up the handbrake outside the shop, I survey the scene before getting out of the car. At 12 o'clock, through the rain beginning to pepper the windscreen, there's a stocky man being dragged down the street by a muzzled, vicious looking bull-mastiff that has a torso like a cage fighter and tattoos of his owner on his back. I wait until they're long gone before getting out of the car. Whilst I do, I jump out of my skin when I hear a knock on the passenger side window.

'Got a cigg-eh, pal?' the swaying, drunken man asks, holding a pretend cigarette to pursed lips.

'Sorry, mate, don't smoke,' I shout back through the window, waggling a finger.

He says nothing, then zigzags off in the direction of a caged, concrete five-a-side football pitch across the road. I wait a little longer until the coast is clear of drunks, dangerous dogs and BMX bandits before getting out of the car.

When I do, I quicken my step towards the shop entrance. Stepping inside, I hear someone bark, 'I'd shoot the lot of them. Bloody bastards!'

I hope the small, plump man behind the counter talking on the phone in an Indian accent isn't talking about his customers.

'What are you wanting, my friend?' he asks, holding the phone away from his face.

'Eggs, please.'

'Over there,' he says, throwing his head one way while pressing a link of rebellious thin hair back over a balding pate with his phone-free hand.

I scan the aisles. There's dusty, half-empty shelves where it looks like the products are social distancing; rusting fridges; an empty card rack; an unappealing produce section with wilting lettuce leaves, overripe bruising bananas and fading yellow lemons. Now I know what NISA stands for: "Nowt In Sod All."

I wander over to the eggs next to the frozen (in time) food section and feast my eyes upon the price. £2.49 for 12 bloody eggs! No wonder times seem tough for him taking advantage of people like me who'll pay anything for a happy, forgiving spouse.

Upon second, more grateful thoughts, I reflect upon what a great service he's providing to folk in urgent need. In truth, his out of hour eggs keeping Rachel's wooden spoon off my head are priceless.

I check the egg box to make sure they weren't laid in 1979, which is when it looks like the fridges were delivered. To my relief, a generous chicken had only recently shat them out.

Grabbing Rachel's favourite treat, Maltesers, as a peace offering, I make for the counter. As I do, a little hunchbacked lady in a pink head scarf and brown overcoat comes shuffling through the door with both gnarly hands clinging to the shopping trolley she's pushing.

'Good evening, my dear!' says the shopkeeper as he runs from behind the counter to help her with the door. 'Are you wanting to come to my place tonight?' he proposes in an oddly seductive tone. 'Are you needing a Bollywood bonking, hmm?' he asks, closing the door behind her.

I stop by some tins of baked beans for a moment and wonder if I've accidentally walked onto the set of a very strange porno niche – "Trolley Dollies" or something equally perverse.

'It's okay,' he assures me, noticing my eyes blinking in disbelief, 'she is not hearing a bloody thing!'

I say nothing, unsure whether I should laugh at him, report him or counsel him as he follows her down the perishables aisle towards me.

When she stops to examine the label on a tin of chopped tomatoes, he stands behind her and does something even more alarming – he pretends to hump her from behind, looking at me while doing it. He's waiting for me to laugh. Waiting for my approval. He's not going to stop thrusting his crotch at her until I acknowledge what he's doing, with some form of amusement.

Even as the lady continues down the aisle, nudging her squeaking shopping trolley-cum-Zimmer frame past me, he thrusts at her from behind her with gritted teeth, fists clenched and screwed up sex face. It's the weirdest thing I've ever witnessed. He gets way too close to me for comfort as they pass, her pigeon-stepping past the tins of peas, sweetcorn and tuna, him thrusting at her brown overcoat. Does he always do this or is he only performing such a weird act for my benefit? More importantly, do I look like the kind of man that would think it's okay to ghost up behind grannies and perform such a lewd act? I certainly hope not!

I'll have to get a cap that clearly states my position on this matter: "I don't approve of feigning fornication with grannies. Buy them fridge magnets from your holidays instead," I'll get written on it.

Praying the lady doesn't turn around and get a heart attack, I force a hollow laugh and flick my thumbs up in the hope that'll make him stop. Thankfully, this does the trick and he leaves the frail little lady in peace.

Slipping back behind the counter, he scans my eggs.

'Bloody Aldi bastards making these one pound 99,' he complains. 'If I'm making this price, I'm shitting the eggs myself to make money!'

'Must be hard,' I sympathise.

'It is. Bloody bastards,' he rues. 'West Ham, is it?' He points at the badge on my jacket, changing the subject.

'My first love,' I say.

'Bloody Bolton bastards always down the bottom, innit,' he complains some more.

'As a West Ham fan, I feel your pain,' I say, presenting my card to pay for the eggs and Maltesers.

'Cash only, my friend,' he insists.

Luckily, I have some on me. As I fish around in my wallet for some change, he asks if it's okay for the lady who's done well to make it round the shop in one piece to go in front of me.

'Of course,' I say, stepping aside.

'Thank you,' the old lady graciously accepts.

She puts some milk, beetroot and biscuits on the counter, then hands him her purse. He opens it and counts out the coins on the counter for her to see. She's 35p short.

I fear he's about to insist that she platt his nipple hairs to make up for the lack of funds. To my relief, he doesn't. Instead, the shopkeeper scoops up the money already on the counter and says, 'Oh look. You're having just the right money, my dear.'

'Thank you,' the lady murmurs.

As she drops the goods into her shopping trolley, the mad shopkeeper comes out from behind the counter again to hold the door for her. Ever so slowly, she doddles out of the shop to the sound of her creaking shopping trolley wheels.

'Take care on the way home, my dear,' he says, then makes his way back to the counter.

As he does, through the glass door, I spy the lady whip off her head scarf, then run off at full speed, giving him the middle finger.

'Wouldn't it be funny if that were true?' I say to Rachel back home in the kitchen as she crowns her grandad's birthday cake with candles.

'Least he turned out to be a good egg after all,' Rachel replies, taking a photo.

Chapter 7

I Short You Not!

Did you know your chances of getting injured by a toilet are one in 10,000? Were you aware that 4% of lost TV remote controls turn up in the freezer? Did you have any inkling that only 8% of December days where I live in the north are sunny?

Today however is not one of those days, my friends. It's cold! We're talking colder-in-the-bedroom-than-in-the-fridge-when-you-wake-up type cold. We're talking shrieking-in-cold-arse-shock-when-posterior-meets-porcelain type cold. We're talking the kind of cold that makes Rachel insist Pearl wrap up in a bright orange fleeced jacket as we're about to leave the house.

'I'm not going out in public with my dog wearing that,' I protest, stamping my feet.

'Why not?' Rachel counters, fastening a buckle under Pearl's belly. 'She looks cute.'

'She looks like she works for motorway maintenance,' I grumble.

'I spent seven pounds on it in Home Bargains, so you have to use it.' Rachel stands firm and takes a picture with her phone.

'Aww, Pearl's first day at work,' I comment, my words dripping in sarcasm.

'Aww, Bradley's last day alive,' she says, switching the focus of the lens onto me. 'Any last requests?' she grants.

'Can I take a photo of Pearl's first winter turd, too?' I say, clipping the lead onto Pearl's collar.

'You are a turd,' Rachel says, kissing me on the lips before going upstairs to get ready for work.

The instant I open the front door, my eyes water from the blast of cold air that slaps me in the face. The warm breath blowing out of my mouth into the frosty air looks like a smoke machine as I take a right out of our driveway and make for where we can safely cross the dual carriageway running past our house with the help of our local lollipop lady.

'So . . . you're Brad,' our lollipop lady says with a finger in the air, recalling our first meeting weeks back. 'And that lady I've seen you with, what's she called?'

'That's my wife, Rachel.'

'With or without an "a"?' she asks.

'Without.'

'Great! I'll pop a Christmas card through't door,' she promises.

'Your name?' I ask.

'Hooorp.'

'Nice to put a face to a name, Hope!' I say as she picks up her lollipop to escort Pearl and me across the road busy with commuter and school run traffic.

We have to stop halfway across on a pedestrian island between the two lanes of traffic going in opposite directions, because a speeding car ignores her big red stop sign.

'Supposed stop, y'bastard,' she spits at the inconsiderate motorist zooming past us.

As the next driver approaches, Hope's eyes turn red and steam billows out of her nose and ears. Threatening to jam the reverse end of her lollipop through the windscreen of the oncoming vehicle, the driver, knowing what's good for him, hits the brakes and lets us cross.

'Ave a nice day, loovies.' Hope waves Pearl and me off before shooting the driver a look that says, 'Don't fucking mess with me and my lollipop.'

This is only the second time I've met Hope, but matters not! This will be the first time I'll receive a Christmas card from a lollipop lady in my life.

True to her word, days later a card drops through our letterbox containing her phone number ("if we ever want to pop in for a brew or need a dog sitter") and a bone-shaped biscuit for Pearl.

Though my heart is warmed by Hope's thoughtfulness and a little disturbed by the punishment she's capable of dishing out to drivers who dare to defy her, my body is still in shock from a bitterly cold morning that's made my testicles shrivel like out-of-date dates.

Pulling my snood up to the bridge of my nose and my West Ham hat down over my forehead so my eyes are the only part of my body unclothed, I fret about how I'm going to make it through my first northern winter. December has only just got out the ice blocks. I've got four more freezing months of this!

After saying our thank yous to Hope for helping us cross the road, Pearl drags me over to the first frost-hardened patch of grass we encounter, then sniffs around, finds her spot and arches her back like an angry alley cat. This is always an awkward moment. You've got to be careful not to watch for too long or appear to be too interested just in case you look like you've got some strange faecal fetish. You must, however, keep a close eye on where the lozenge is laid, just in case you can't find it hiding in the grass. I wouldn't want my new neighbours thinking I'm not a pooper scooper.

Sometimes, if her stool is being stubborn, Pearl makes intense eye contact in the act like she's asking for help. It's as if she wants me to give it pep talk and coax it out like a bird feeder might a sparrow from a tree top. There's no way I'm going to enter into negotiations with her temperamental sphincter for the release of Pearl's butt biscuits. Not in front of new neighbours, anyway. I have to let Pearl deal with this one alone, so I break eye contact with her, look away and scan the streets. In the cul-de-sac opposite, a fleet of workmen in high-vis orange jackets similar to Pearl's are steamrolling the road. A gloved-up, track-suited morning runner sporting a beanie cheek-puffs past me. A sledgehammer-wielding block paver pounds a driveway. A Jack Russell yaps at us from behind a living room window, its helicoptering tail thudding against the window pane.

As the bitter smell of hot, freshly laid tar floats over and stings the back of my throat, I wonder if the steamrollers are going to offer Pearl a job with her matching high-vis worker's jacket.

Come the time to finally bag up Pearl's rectum rusks, a builder emerges from a bungalow behind me undergoing renovations.

'You can leave that in my skip if you want, pal,' he says in a cheerful, nothing-is-too-much-trouble tone.

'Thanks, mate!'

That's how friendly I'm finding people up here. They offer you use of their skips for shits and send you Christmas cards when you hardly know them.

I could get used to this! I think as I take the builder up on his kind offer.

Across the street, I overhear a mum drilling her kids on their spellings on their walk to school.

'Almost,' she challenges.

'A-l-m-o-s-t,' answers her little boy correctly.

'Well done! Brilliant! Always . . .'

'A-l-w-a-y-s,' her little girl responds.

During that brutal and mentally challenging first Spanish lockdown, I read an article suggesting that the first emotion you feel in the morning can make or break the rest of your day. Bearing witness to that sweet and heartwarming spelling test certainly makes mine.

After reading that article, I set my alarm to play my favourite U2 song, "Beautiful Day," so I feel pleasure instead of panic when I first wake up. So the first words I hear prime my thoughts and set a positive tone for the rest of the day. It really does make a difference and I highly recommend you do so, too. Unless your favourite song is "Burning Down the House," then you might as well use a fire alarm to wake up.

With Pearl's business finally complete, we begin our expedition back home through the streets of Antarctica. That's what it feels like, anyway, in comparison to where I lived in Tenerife where the lowest winter temperature was a balmy 16 degrees. As we pass some penguins, polar bears and a yeti, a crazy character across the street catches my eye – a madman casually strolling the frosty streets like he's heading to the seaside in summer. How is this possible? How can this freak of nature survive wearing what I wore almost every day in Tenerife – only shorts, vest and flip flops – when I'm still cold even though I'm currently wearing long johns under my hiking trousers, two pairs of socks, a vest, a t-shirt, a roll neck jumper, a hoodie, my big coat, a snood, a scarf and two (yes, two) pairs of gloves?

I can only assume he's been thrown out of his house by his other half, lost a bet with his mates, or trying to compete with me in the Stiffest Nipples On The Street competition.

Just looking at him in his summer holiday clobber walking the wintry streets makes me feel even colder. I tell Pearl to pick up the pace so we can get back home and spend the day inside the oven.

As I'm about to turn the corner to our house, I'm waved down by an elderly gentleman from the doorstep of his bungalow across the road.

'Excuse me, have you got a minute?' he shouts.

I stare straight ahead and continue walking, pretending I haven't heard. In the corner of my eye, I catch him walking up his drive to pursue me.

''Ere!' he shouts. 'Sorry to trouble you, but can you help me?'

I reluctantly stop but keep my guard up just in case he's up to something. Have "the others" who were coming back to "see me again" finally caught up with me?

'Like I said, so sorry to trouble you,' says a man in a brown dressing gown and grey slippers, leaning on a walking stick. 'I just need help to move a big table out of me living room,' he says, pointing back inside his house. 'I'm having new carpet put in.'

'What about my dog?' I ask, hoping Pearl can be my get-out clause, my excuse for not having to go into this stranger's house.

'Your dog can come in too,' he says. 'No bother.'

Heeding the man's call for help, I cautiously enter his house, leave Pearl in the landing, then step into his living room where, sure enough, there's a huge glass table upside down on the floor, legs in the air.

'I tried do it meself, but it's too heavy for me,' he says.

'I'll do my best,' I pledge, taking off my two pairs of gloves and rolling my coat sleeves up.

After a bit of heave-hoing, I manage to ease it sideways through a door leading to the kitchen so the old carpet can be taken up and the new one can be laid.

'Thanks ever so much,' the man says when we leave.

'Will you need help to put it back once the carpet's been laid?' I ask.

'I'll get carpet fitters to do that. You've already done more than enough. Thanks so much again,' he says.

Once back home, it dawns on me how suspicious I still am of people. All the guy wanted was a little help and here I was worrying that he wanted to kidnap me. I had fears that he'd offer me a poisoned cup of tea, then I'd wake up in his basement where Beryl would be there force-feeding me her bunions and foot corn until I told them the code to my online bank account. Failing that, they'd bring in the Barry White bus lady, waving her cheese toasty in my face until I gave in. If that didn't work, they'd get the big-bottomed barmy lady to force-feed me butter until I could take no more.

Popping the kettle on to fill up a hot water bottle, I am struck by how trusting the man was to invite me, a complete stranger he didn't know from Adam, into his house. This is a level of trust in one's fellow citizens I've rarely been exposed to in everyday life, and an example once again of how warm, open and friendly the locals are. It's still taking some getting used to, but I have to admit, I'm really beginning to like it.

Later that same freezing week, I meet with a friend of mine. I can't give you his real name because he's a policeman so I thought of one that sounds northern – Tarquin. Somewhat rudely, I forget to say hello and instead pass comment at the bare flesh he has on show.

'How are you not dying of hypothermia?' I say, pointing at Tarquin's exposed legs poking out of his shorts.

'Like summer, this!' he says, mock wiping his brow. 'I'm sweating cobs, me!'

To the tune of a tinkling, rock-strewn stream racing us alongside a serpentine, undulating path of crunchy leaves, we set off on a dog walk. Under a canopy of gnarly branches stripped by winter of its foliage, Pearl is chasing squirrels on their final forage for hibernation, and Tarquin's inexhaustible cocker spaniel puppy Riley is bounding here, there and everywhere.

When we reach the top of some steps and prepare to descend, we cross paths with a senior gentlemen who's just walked up them. He's dressed like most sane people in winter and, like me, actually treated his legs to the comfort of a pair of trousers. He's even put on a coat. This elder statesman, this wise owl who probably has some southern blood given his choice of warm clothing, makes me feel better about the fact that I've gone on a dog walk insulated once again with more layers than a lasagne.

'Someone's left bloomin' light on,' he says, pointing at the weak mid-afternoon sun barely visible through the thick cloud blanketing the winter sky. 'Hot, int'it?' he complains, unzipping his fleece down from chin to chest.

'Told you,' says Tarquin before blowing a whistle so Riley comes bouncing back to him from somewhere deep in the forest. 'It's roasting!'

A few days later, when Saturday morning comes, the weather is roasting again – two degrees Celsius, just as it was the day of the dog walk. When the postman knocks early doors and asks me to sign for a delivery, I stare at his legs and am inspired by his gung-ho, can-do, nothing-will-stop-me-wearing-my-summer-shorts attitude. Even if, as touched on at the start of this chapter, the sun is predicted to shine up here in the northwest for just 58 of December's 720 hours. Our postman is an optimist. A glass 8% full kind of guy.

Closing my front door, package in hand, I vow to change my ways. I shall fit in with my new neighbours. After all, what must they think of me, leaving the house looking like the time I once boarded a plane wearing most of the clothes in my suitcase to protest Ryanair's extortionate excess weight charges? I was padded up like a police dog trainer.

I will feel this shame no more, I declare as I clip the lead onto Pearl and hit the cold, wet and misty streets. I stick my chest out, hold my chin up and hope the neighbourhood notices the brave and bold move I've made. I too have bare flesh on show. I've taken my gloves off.

One step at a time, eh?

Chapter 8

Eau de Toilette

Today is going to be the day. That's right! After a nine-month absence thanks to Covid restrictions and relocation upheavals, I'm finally going to get back in the gym because great news has broken: lockdown has been lifted!

2 p.m. is the start of my hour-long slot. Or so I thought, until the plumber calls and puts a spanner in the works.

'I'll be there half-one-ish,' the plumber estimates.

Then the dog groomer's on the phone.

'Can fit you in at one?' Sharon from A Mutt Above proposes.

I've changed the groomer's and the company's names so they don't sue me, given the bombshell about them I'm about to drop.

'You're cutting my dog's hair, not mine,' I joke.

'I'll be cutting our ties if you keep telling those bad jokes. I'll not be long, loov!' she says, hanging up.

Cutting to the chase, I'm now cutting it fine for my gym appointment at 2pm. That's now the end of the "cut" puns, by the way. Any more I think of will be left on the cutting room floor. Sorry, I couldn't resist that last one. I'll cut it out now.

It's just my luck that on the day I had an early finish from work and planned to start burning off my lockdown love handles, the groomer and the plumber are both available again at long last after they had to postpone the previous appointments I'd had because of the ever-changing lockdown restrictions. I can't even call Rachel for help because she's at work. The law of sod is officially passed in the houses of the bloody typical.

I revise my day's itinerary . . .

If the groomer can be done by half one and the plumber is quick, I can still be flexing my pigeon chest in the gym mirrors not long after 2pm. Long as they're both on time.

They're not! A Mutt Above rocks up 25 precious, infuriating and frustrating minutes late. I'm more annoyed than when a whole biscuit broke in my tea at breakfast.

'Sorry, loov,' Sharon apologises, dropping her doggy bags on the carpet in the living room.

'Last job were big labby – hair everywhere.'

Despite her tardiness, Sharon, wearing a black anorak with "A Mutt Above" written in white letters on the back, takes a casual five to 10 minutes flicking hair off her razors onto a mat with a comb whilst making small talk. Maybe this is why she was late? Faffing. Gabbing. Hair flicking. Come on, Sharon, let's get shearing!

Continuing her preparation in a slow, measured and painstaking fashion, Sharon sets up a portable table, lays down a towel, unravels an extension lead and plugs in her electric razor. Just as I think the grooming is about to get going, she has another little sit-down.

Come on, come on.

'You're not from reauwnd 'ere, are you?' she unsurprisingly asks.

'How'd you guess?' I reply.

'You sound like 'im off telly. What's his name? Danny Dyer.'

'If we didn't have thumbs, we couldn't eat sandwiches,' I say, doing my best Danny Dyer impression.

'You what, love?'

'That's one of his most famous lines,' I inform her.

'Oh right. I thought you'd gone mad f'moment. And, where'd ya get this little black beauty from?' she asks, pointing at Pearl who's sat next to her on the sofa with her head buried between her back legs, licking her six nipples.

I get an urge to ignore the question and say: 'Get on with it, Shazza. Us southerners don't do this pointless, idle chatter thing. If we haven't got a gym appointment to go to, we're on the lookout for dangerous people like Danny Dyer does in his programme, *Deadliest Men*.'

Remembering my manners, I refrain from being rude, then politely reply and give her the short version of Pearl's long backstory.

I tell her about how we soon found out after rescuing Pearl that she was dying of heart worms; about how a series of arsenic injections that could kill the worms and cure her but also potentially kill her was Pearl's only chance of surviving; about how we had to carry her around in a bag during her treatment because she was too weak to walk; and about how she came through the treatment and is now fit, healthy and badly needing her first groom in nearly a year because she looks like Dog Marley.

After telling Pearl's tale, I stand up from the armchair next to Sharon, dropping a not-so-subtle hint that it's time for the cutting to commence.

'How could anyone abandon this little love?' she says, patting Pearl on the head, not getting the hint.

'Some heartless buggers out there,' I say.

'Mind if I use your loo before I get started, Bradley?' she asks, getting up from the sofa and unbuckling the belt on her jeans.

For dog sake!

''Course not. Top of the stairs.'

While Sharon is in the toilet, there's a knock at the door – must be the plumber! I check my watch. He's late, too! Ten blood-boiling minutes late.

I've now got only 20 minutes before my gym slot. Twenty minutes during which the plumber has to plumb, the groomer has to groom, and I've got to somehow hurry them both along without appearing like the impatient southerner that I am who's double busy and has places to go, people to see and iron to pump in the gym.

By the front door at the bottom of our stairs, I introduce the plumber to the groomer.

'Ow do?' he says, clanging a metal toolbox onto the floor.

'You alright, love?' she says, doing up her belt.

Pearl comes to greet the plumber, too.

'What a lovely little dog,' he says, ruffling the fur on her head. 'They're just the best pals, aren't they?'

'Certainly are,' I agree. 'Shall I show you wh –'

'Ours just recently passed,' he laments, swallowing a lump in his throat.

'It's just so 'ard when they're' – he breaks off and takes a few seconds to compose himself – 'not by your side anymore.'

Now I feel bad for cursing him for being late. He seems really nice.

'Come here,' says Sharon, pulling him close. 'Sod all that no-hugging Covid stuff.'

He relaxes in her arms and starts to sob.

As she passes him a tissue from a pocket, a suffocating, excremental scent alarms my nostrils. Makes them flare. Makes me wretch and forget for a moment that the plumber, bless him, is having a moment.

This must be Sharon's *eau de toilette*. She's not only gone to the toilet. Sharon's had a shit! What the hell? Is that what people do up here? They're all so open and friendly and comfortable in each other's company that they just casually stroll into other people's houses and defecate?

Is this just another of those unique northern quirks like saying hello to strangers, sticking butter everywhere and listing your ailments when you first meet someone?

I worry about what the plumber's next move might be. Is he going to go have a lie-down in our bed because he's had a long day? Use my toothbrush? Take a piss in the garden?

What if he thinks it's me and not Sharon that's sentenced him to work in a toilet that smells like a family-sized bag of salt and vinegar crisps? He'll probably assume I've left a pan pie up there for him in revenge for turning up late.

I pray she flushed. Oh no! What if Mrs Mutt Above left a floater? The plumber's going to charge me double and slap his own tax on top – V.A.T. (Very Awful Turd).

I suspect Sharon might have done, because Pearl has gone to the top of the stairs and is sniffing at the toilet door with great interest. I call her back down the stairs when at long last I hear Sharon's razors buzz into action in the living room.

'The leak's just behind the cistern,' I say to the plumber, pointing upstairs to the bathroom. 'You'll see where I've put a bucket to collect the water.'

With sad, pining-for-his-dead-dog eyes, he looks at me for reassurance before going up.

Unfortunately, I can't offer any as I try and fail to unsmell Sharon's shit.

He hesitantly walks up the stairs and into the toilet. He's out inside a minute.

'Ran out of pipe repair tape,' he claims, gasping for breath and closing the door behind him. 'I'll 'aff come back.'

He never did. Neither did I get to the gym or eat a packet of salt n' vinegar crisps again.

Chapter 9

Much Ado About Something . . .

At first, I think I'm being paranoid. Surely those four people huddled in the corner by the swimming pool changing rooms, surreptitiously pointing in my general direction, can't be talking about me, right?

I double-check about my person. I've no verrucas I need to bazooka. I don't have a testicle hanging out of my swim shorts. Neither do my trunks have any suspect stains. All appears to be in order and everything in its place.

That said, it seems I must have done something to attract unwanted attention, because as much as I try to reassure myself that it's just my imagination, I'm definitely being talked about. Discussed. The topic of hushed conversation. I'm the reason why chins are being wagged, heads scratched and brows furrowed deep in thought.

Maybe word has got around and they've mistaken me as the southerner in town who purposely poops when he knows the plumber is coming to inspect his toilet? Maybe they're going to come over and tell me that swimming floats will be tolerated but floaters will not upon any circumstances?

Whatever the reason, it's my presence that's causing a fuss. A small, bald and overweight lifeguard in yellow shorts and a red t-shirt breaks off from the group. He's coming over.

'Scuse me, pal,' he says. 'What's that thing you've got there?'

'Do you mean this?' I say, pointing to the manbun that's wobbling about on the top of my head. 'Yeah sorry, lockdown locks. I'm gonna get it cut off soon.'

'No. Not your hair!' he says. 'That thing. What is it?'

'What. This?' I say, tapping the article protruding up from my forehead like a periscope. 'My snorkel?'

'Yeah. That. You can't use it in 'ere.'

'Why?' I protest, grabbing onto it protectively with both hands.

'You just can't. It's the rules.'

'But why? I've used this in loads of swimming pools,' I point out. 'No one has ever told me I can't use it.'

'Fair enough,' he says, then returns to the committee watching on from the corner.

Well this is VERY weird. One minute I just can't use it. It's the rules. Scary pointy fingers. Next minute – fair enough.

They're going to want to go over their vague, unsubstantiated, flakey rules before creating such scenes and making me feel like an idiot in front of my fellow swimmers, many of whom had stopped to listen in on our conversation.

I never had these trivial problems in Tenerife. Pre-pandemic, me and my snorkel could swim hassle free amongst schools of fish in crystal clear waters warmed by glorious sunshine. Now, as I resume my lengths, I'm being given a guilt trip for using it as countless flakey particles of dead skin, pubic hair and the odd plaster float past my goggles.

Even back home down south, when visiting friends and family, my snorkel and I were always left in peace by the lifeguards when I went swimming.

Why is it such a problem up here? I bemoan as I slalom two grannies who've stopped to have a chat in the shallow end.

'Oooh, he loovs me gammon steak, he does,' one of them says, poking some hair back under her swimming hat.

A few minutes later, out of the corner of my eye, I see the snorkel police have reconvened in the corner. This time there's five of them. One more than before – a new man who's wearing the trousers because he's not just the manager, he's THE DUTY MANAGER. He's always wearing a shirt and tie as well as the managerial trousers. This is getting silly.

He furtively tilts his head and moves his eyes in my direction to confirm with his colleagues that it's me that's the troublemaker.

Affirmative.

A lady who was at the reception desk when I entered the building says the word, 'manbun.'

He's coming over . . . Here we go again.

'Excuse me, sir. Can I have a look at your snorkel, please?'

I pretend I haven't heard him and continue swimming in mute protest. He follows me down to the deep end of the pool and asks again, shouting this time.

Arms resting on the poolside, I harrumph the snorkel off my head and present it for examination.

He looks it up and down like a mad scientist might a bubbling test tube.

'You're not allowed to use these.'

'But why?'

'You can't have anything obstructing your face while you swim.'

'It's not obstructing my face,' I argue. 'It's actually helping me swim. Look, it even says "Speedo" on it. It's actually made for swimming in swimming pools.'

The grannies gassing about gammon in the shallow end look shocked and stop talking. Maybe they've misheard and think I've said paedo, not Speedo. I want to shout across the pool, 'Don't worry, girls, I'm not a paedo wearing Speedos and I've got a valid DBS check to prove it,' but think again. That'll only make this awkward situation, this kerfuffle, this much ado about nothing, even more uncomfortable.

Making eye contact with the grannies, I run my finger over the letters running down the snorkel whilst slowly and silently mouthing the syllables – "Spee-do." They break eye contact and look away.

'Why do you need to use it, anyway?' the duty manager asks, handing it back to me.

'Eh?'

'What do you need the snorkel for?'

I mean, come on. I'm using a snorkel in a swimming pool. It's not like I've walked in here in a shark costume and started chasing people around the pool, nipping at their ankles while singing the Jaws theme tune.

I have to think back for a moment to why I first started using a snorkel when swimming many moons ago.

'Erm. I've got scoliosis, a curvature of the spine. It helps me keep it aligned and tone the muscles supporting it,' I feel the need to explain.

'Fair enough,' he says, and saunters off to rejoin the staff members, lifeguards and first aid mannequins looking on.

Part of me thinks I should just get out of the pool because my fellow swimmers now suspect I'm a Speedo-wearing paedo, heavy-breathing through a snorkel so I can get a better look at them underwater. But no. I know my rights and I've waited months for the pool to reopen again after lockdown, and I shall complete my 64 lengths. I also know I'm a respectable new member of this community who won't be bullied into taking off his snorkel.

I resume my lengths, paranoid that everyone is trying to swim away from me. For around 10 minutes, I'm left alone. That is, until I arrive at the poolside in the deep end and hear a muffled voice from underwater. I lift my head above the surface.

'Can I have a word, please?'

HEAD LIFEGUARD, his badge says. "Jobsworth" would be a better title.

'If you've got a spinal injury, you shouldn't be int' pool,' he orders.

'It's NOT an injury,' I whinge again. 'It's just a hereditary condition. My physio told me to use it.'

'Have you got a letter to prove it?'

'What, like from my mum? Not to do PE?' I sarcastically reply with a not-so-private tut.

'No, I mean a doctor's or physio's note, anything like that?'

'Um . . . I should have a copy of the MRI results in my emails.'

'Can you come to reception and show us before you leave so we can put a note on your file?'

Begrudgingly, I do just that. Accessing my emails on my smartphone, I find the message with the MRI results attached.

'Fair enough,' the Duty Manager says from behind the plastic Covid screen in the reception area. 'We've put a note on your file.'

I walk away from the leisure centre into the inky black December night, attacked from all angles by a manic rain, incredulous.

In the same part of the world where so many world firsts were pioneered (world's first intercity passenger railway, Manchester to Liverpool, 1830; world's first submarine, Manchester, 1878; world's first contraceptive pill, University of Manchester, 1961), a snorkel, a swimming accessory being used in a swimming pool, is too hard a concept for certain staff members to fathom. A mind bender. Too much for them to wrap their heads around.

As I'm about stick my key in the front door, my phone rings.

'Mr Kermie-side?' a female voice checks.

'Um. It's actually CH-ermside.'

'Says Kermie-side 'ere.'

'Kermie-side. Chermside. Doesn't matter. Kids used to call me Mr Circumcised when I was a PE teacher.' I regret saying that last sentence as soon as it spills out of my mouth. Time, place and all that.

'This is Denise from't leisure centre. Just calling to let you know . . . you've left your snorkel int' changing rooms.'

'That's really nice of you to let me know,' I say, immediately feeling bad for losing my patience with them earlier. 'I'll come back and get it in the morning.'

At reception the next day, there's a lady who wasn't there the night before. She hands me back the snorkel. I assume she's forgotten to take off the post-it note that has written on it:

"Soft southerner coming to pick up today."

The last laugh, quite rightly, is on me.

Chapter 10

Tail Wind

Rachel is obsessed with dating programmes. She watches the lot – *Dinner Date*. *First Dates*. *Secret Crush*. *Love Bites*. *Dress to Impress*. *The Undateables*.

I come up with an idea for one more while she's watching *First Dates* and I'm on the floor doing press-ups.

'Wouldn't it be funny,' I say to Rachel, 'if, instead of *First Dates*, they made a programme called *Worst Dates*?'

'No, it wouldn't,' she disagrees, then 'awws' at a cute elderly couple getting on famously.

'It would,' I insist. 'They could purposely match people who they think wouldn't get on. Like a feminist with a chauvinist. A butcher with a vegan. It'd be carnage.'

'Stop ruining it,' she says as the singletons in their 80s hug and agree they'd like to see each other again.

"I'd love to come see your flowers," the old man beams with a twinkle in his eyes. (That's not a euphemism, he really does want to see the flowers in her rose garden.)

'I love his chivalry,' Rachel says as the suited and booted elderly chap holds a taxi door open for the lady.

'Or,' I say, still droning on about my stupid idea, 'they could set people up. Have actors play one-half of the date. They could have a guy who's Pac-Man mad turning up wearing a Pac-Man t-shirt and have him making a sound effect every time he puts food in his mouth.'

'Dwing,' I demonstrate by popping one of Rachel's grapes in my mouth.

'Or,' I drone on, 'they could have a woman turn up with bright green snot hanging out of one nostril. She could break the ice by asking, "How's it hanging?"'

'They could also pair an annoying southerner who won't stop talking rubbish with a northerner who's running out of patience,' Rachel warns me, turning the telly up to drown me out. She then has to turn it straight back down again because the phone rings. It's her mum. She's got a proposal for us: now that some lockdown restrictions have been eased, would we like to be appointed as trusted members of Grandad Stanley's official support bubble? Of course we bloody would! What an honour!

If you're reading this long after the Covid pandemic of the early 2020s and have no idea what I'm talking about, a support bubble is two households that are legally allowed to enter into the house of one other to help them, their purpose being to help those in need who've been cut off from friends and family.

I was a little disappointed I didn't get a uniform, hat or badge to show off this elevation in my social status, but matters not. The most important thing is that we can now go into Stanley's house without fear of being fined or the neighbours snitching on us. Strange days indeed but exciting times nonetheless.

Next day, Stanley's on the phone as soon as he hears the news that we can come into his house for the first time since we returned home.

'There's a draught int' living room making me feet cold,' he says.

Assuming the role of Draught Detectives, we jump in the car and head over on a Tuesday evening after work.

His golden retriever, Millie, barks as we approach his front door and ring the bell. "We Wish You a Merry Christmas" plays as always, but this time, in season. A light switches on in the hallway. The inviting smell of toast wafts out of the kitchen when he opens the door.

'Waheeeeey!' he cheers like he always does when sees us. Millie is equally pleased, her big tail whipping happy helicopters.

Following him inside, we get a welcome blast from the central heating like the opening of an oven door. It brings back memories of the warm air that used to kiss our faces when we got off the plane in Tenerife, after trips back to Blighty. Them's were the days, eh?

Rachel and I begin peeling off our winter layers as Stanley tells us about his new clock.

'It's a good'un,' he says, pointing at his new timekeeper mounted on the wall above the fireplace. 'Keeps great time, it does. It's not missed a bloomin' second, so far.'

'Good bit of kit that, Stanley,' I chime, acknowledging Stanley's new clock.

His liking for clock-watching reminds me of Rachel's fondness for watching clothes dry.

'I find it therapeutic,' she said when I first caught her staring in wonder at washing hanging on the line.

'Would you like some toast?' Stanley offers. 'I'm that hungry, me belly thinks me throat's been cut.'

'I'm okay thanks, Stanley. What about that draught making your feet cold?' I remind him.

'Oh yeah. So, when I'm sat 'ere watching football' – he points to his armchair in front of the TV, flanked by a wooden sideboard decorated with Best Grandad coasters, framed pictures of the grandchildren, and his late wife, Stella – 'there's a draught making me feet cold.'

'I'll have a gander for you,' I promise.

I get straight to work while Rachel goes into the kitchen with Stanley to make a cuppa, get the toast on and have a natter. I dive behind the front living room curtains and check the windows closest to his armchair. All seems airtight with the double glazing seals. I close the living room door and feel around the bottom of it for cold air. None appears to be getting under it. I examine the back windows looking out onto the garden, where a photo of him with Rachel's dad and brother in front of Wembley Stadium's vintage Twin Towers in their Bolton Wanderers shirts graces the windowsill. I feel around the fireplace, too. There's not a breath of air to be found anywhere. I try sitting in Stanley's chair myself to see if I can sense where the cold air might be leaking in from. I try with my socks on and off, but still feel nothing. The draught that Stanley's complaining about doesn't appear to be present.

'Next time you feel it,' I suggest when he comes back into the living room with a plate of toast, 'maybe just put a blanket on your feet?'

'Or, wear those Bolton slippers I bought you for your birthday,' Rachels says, sipping on her brew.

'What, them ones over there?' he says, pointing to the slippers still boxed up under the dining table.

'Yeah. Put them on now,' Rachel suggests and goes to get them.

'Oooh. It's like putting me feet to bed,' he says, wiggling his toes about in his new slippers.

'Talking of Bolton,' Rachel continues. 'I've got something to show you.'

She digs out her phone and shows him a picture. It's a publicity shot from Bolton Wanderers Football Club website. Scribed at the bottom of the image with some fans cheering a goal are the words:

One town. One community. One team.

And who's the man, centre of attention, in the middle of photo? None other than Mr Stanley Lee!

'Look, it's you!' she says, pointing at him in the picture.

'Eh?'

'It's you. Bolton have put a picture up with you in it. You're the star!'

'Oh aye, so I am!' he says, registering his own beaming smile with arms thrown into the air and fists clenched in celebration.

'Eh! We've got some more good news!' Rachel announces and retrieves a video message on her phone recorded by her older brother. He pushes his glasses up his nose and squints to focus. Rachel presses play.

'Hello, Grandad! 'Orp you're okay!' he says.

'Waheey!' Stanley shouts back at the screen. ''Ow you doin'? You coming over?'

Rachel pauses the video.

'It's a video message, not a FaceTime. You can't actually speak to him.'

'Oh, bloomin' 'eck, I thought he were calling.'

'No. It's a video message. Listen, Grandad, he wants tell you summat,' Rachel says, touching a loving hand to his forearm. She presses play again.

'I know we still can't come and see you in person, so just wanted to let you know,' her brother says before building up the tension with a brief, silent pause in which he brings his fiancé on camera. 'You're gonna be a great-grandad! Samantha's expecting.'

Rachel stops the video and we both stare at him in anticipation of his response. Should we get the kettle on again and celebrate with some of his favourite bourbon biscuits? Pop some more toast in? Should we fetch the tissues just in case he tears up? Rock around his new clock doing a celebratory dance?

After a few seconds to process the happy news, he looks at us both like he's had a lightbulb moment.

'She can 'ave some of your nan's pregnancy clothes. I've still got 'em upstairs. They're good'uns.'

'Aww, that's a lovely idea, Grandad,' Rachel agrees.

'She's not having your nan's knickers, though. She's got some belters in a box in the wardrobe.'

'How could we forget!' Rachel laughs, remembering the saucy sauce moment a couple of months back.

''Ere, what size suit are you?' Stanley asks me.

'I don't know,' I say. 'Rachel always buys my clothes for me.'

It's true. If Rachel, who used to work as a stylist at a high fashion brand in Knightsbridge, didn't buy my clothes for me, I'd look like I'd lost my suitcase at an airport and got dressed blindfolded with clothes from lost property.

'He's a large, Grandad,' Rachel says. 'Why?'

'I've got some of your Uncle Buddy's suits upstairs.'

'Uncle Buddy who died last year?' Rachel asks.

'Yeah. Brad'd look smashing in them.'

Not wanting to be rude and refuse the offer to wear Stanley's dead brother-in-law's clothes (no offence if you're reading this up there,

Uncle Buddy!) I steer the conversation to another matter we need to sort out as officers of Team Stanley.

'Do you know you sent me photos of your gas and electricity metres on Facebook the other night?'

'You what?'

I hold up the photos Stanley sent me.

He pushes his glasses up his nose. 'What's them?'

'Your gas and electricity metres.'

'Me what?'

'They're your gas, and e-lec-tri-ci-ty metre readings,' Rachel repeats a little slower and much louder. 'You sent them to Brad.'

'Did I?'

'Yeah!'

'Oh!' he cries, then bursts out laughing at himself. 'I must've 'ad a maze about!'[1]

'Don't worry! We'll show you how to send them properly,' I say.

Keeping my promise, I crawl under the stairs to get his most up-to-date electricity metre reading and lunge on the floor in the garage to do the same for the gas. After that, we sit down at the living room table, download his supplier's application on his phone and slowly guide him through how he can do it for himself in the future.

''Ere,' he says afterwards, waving us to come into the kitchen, 'I've got summat show ya's. I'm making a little hut f'birds,' he says, lifting up a wooden construction sitting on the kitchen top.

'What's the pen for?' I ask.

---

1. A moment of madness. Down south we might say, "lost the plot", "gone round the bend" or "lost one's marbles".

'It's gonna be their perch,' he says. 'I'm gonna poke it through a hole I've drilled int' middle for em' to stand on.'

'Aww. That's nice of you, Grandad.'

'I need cut grass f'robins, too,' he says, mowing the kitchen floor with an imaginary Flymo. 'It's too long for their little legs.'

While we share a cuppa in front of the telly before we leave, his dog Millie comes and lies at my feet and rolls around on the ground for a belly rub. She then goes over to Rachel with a toy in her mouth, ready for a tug-of-war.

It's then that I feel it . . . the draught. It comes and goes. Starts and stops. Varies in strength, intensity and velocity.

'Can you feel the draught now, Stanley?' I quiz him.

He takes his new slippers off to sense what's going on around his feet.

'Yeah, I can! That's it!'

I check around to see what's changed since the last inspection half an hour or so ago. Curtains. Windows. Fireplace. Doors. All appears to be the same. Rachel stops trying to wrestle the toy from Millie's mouth to zero in on the root of the problem.

I ask Stanley to turn the TV down. The sound of Millie's tail whipping the carpet in excited anticipation of Rachel resuming the tug-of-war is now the loudest. I call her over to come sit at my feet and calm down. (Millie, not Rachel. That would be grounds for divorce).

Millie is now completely still. Interestingly, the draught is no longer palpable.

Performing a new test, I wave the toy around to get her excited. Her tail starts up again.

'It's back again!' Stanley says, scanning the room for the source of the cold air.

I stop playing. Her tail stops wagging.

'What about now?' I ask.

'That's funny int'it?' he observes. 'Gone.'

'It's the dog's tail,' I say to Stanley.

'You what?'

'That's what's causing the draught. Millie's tail.'

'You might be right.'

'I am. Watch.' I repeat the test I conducted seconds earlier.

'Aye, so you are.'

As we settle into conversation before leaving, Millie remains hungry for attention. She comes to me with the toy in her mouth, tail flapping.

Stanley takes off a Bolton Wanderers slipper and gently places it on her tail to plug the draft.

First mission in Team Stanley accomplished!

Chapter 11

Cold Pie, Warm Pasty

'Pasty and peas?' an older gent says to Rachel and me as we're strolling in our local park late afternoon, approaching us from behind and taking us by surprise. We don't quite get what he's getting at. I silently wonder if "Pasty and Peas" are nicknames he's given us.

'Sorry?' I say to the man wearing a tweed flat cap.

'We just bought pasty and peas from't chippy,' he says, holding up a carrier bag full of takeaway containers.

'Oh, right,' I say, still uncertain why he's telling us this.

'Would you and your lovely lady like them? The wife's already full.' He points to a woman wearing matching white woolly hat, scarf and gloves, sitting on a park bench just a pea's throw away.

'I told her not to eat too many chips,' he says, eyes to the heavens like she never learns her lesson. 'She's got no room left f'pasty or peas.'

'Thanks!' I say. 'That's really kind of you.'

The charming man hands over the goods. We look like we've just done a dodgy deal in a local park in broad daylight. A chippy bag disguising a delivery of contraband.

Once he's out of earshot back on the park bench next to his wife, Rachel prods me as I peer excitedly into the bag and sniff at its contents.

'Do NOT even think about it, Bradley Chermside!'

'Why? It's just gonna go to waste otherwise.'

'Covid!'

'Covid, schmovid,' I dismiss her concerns and walk away in defiance with my pasty and peas.

I look back to the old man on the bench who gives me a smile that says, "You're very welcome, my southern friend." His wife waves, then pats her stomach in the universal gesture for "I've eaten a horse and gone back f'jockey."

I lift the bag in gratitude.

Although Rachel, ever the voice of reason, has a very valid point, I'm still refusing to part ways with my pasty and peas. They smell nice. We've grown close in the short time we've known each other. We've bonded. And, it's only now after so long living abroad that I realise how much I've missed this feeling. This home comfort of warming my cold hands on hot takeaway containers. On a parky afternoon in the park at last light, it's a very welcome source of heat.

'You can put it in that bin over there, where they won't see you,' Rachel says, bringing my attention to a bin ahead with its mouth open, hungry for rubbish.

I stay silent, cradle the bag to my chest and look for a bush where I can run and hide from her, then gobble it up.

'Bradley Chermside!' she warns, wagging an authoritative finger at me.

Good job I love her and she's only bossy like this when it's for my own good.

'Throw it away and then clean your hands with this,' she orders, retrieving a mini bottle of hand sanitiser from her handbag.

Mumbling childish complaints under my breath, I do as I'm told. I make a mental note about which bin I just put it in (the one by the bowling green) and hatch a plan in my head to sneak out in the middle of the night and come back and get it when she's sleeping. A few minutes in a microwave can fix this. She's won the battle, but not the war!

We continue ambling through our leafy, local park under swollen black clouds threatening to burst at any moment. Kids are swinging on creaking swings and clambering on climbing frames. Footballs are being kicked and basketballs bounced in a concrete recreation area. Barking dogs are splashing through muddy puddles in the waterlogged grass, chasing balls, sticks and toys thrown by their owners. A hormonal teenager on the way home from school is humping a traffic cone, making very unsettling coital noises, much to the amusement of his giggling friends. A lady wearing a leopard print fur coat and a Russian-style winter hat walks past with Rod Stewart's "Maggie May" playing on her phone. Her overbearing musky perfume is so pungent, I can taste it on the tip of my tongue.

'She's a Glam Gran,' Rachel compliments her.

'Let's go get one,' I say.

'One what?'

'A Glam Gran,' I say sarcastically. 'What do you think I mean? A pasty, of course. That man's made me hungry.'

'I was gonna cook a veggie lasagne when we get home,' Rachel says.

'I. Want. A pasty,' I bawl, standing my ground with my arms crossed, still angry I've been made to part ways with my pasty and peas.

'Only if we go to Greenhalgh's,' Rachel bargains. 'I love their vegan pasties.'

'Deal.'

Moving with renewed pasty-motivated purpose, we cross the park towards the gated exit leading to Greenhalgh's Bakery.

We have 15 minutes until the shutters come down for the day. Just enough time to make it. I tug on Pearl's lead to get her moving a little quicker, too. She's none the wiser of our time-sensitive pasty plans, and still wants to sniff every bush, bench and blade of grass she comes across. That is, until her sniffing comes to an abrupt halt and her ears prick up when she senses danger. I survey the scene. There's no peril, but there's something – someone – even more alarming: Beryl and her bunion! She's walking Dennis, the Irish terrier that terrorised Pearl recently and tried to plant puppies in her in the woods. That's why Pearl's now whining, and why I pick up the pace.

'Quick,' I say to Rachel. 'It's her!'

'Who?'

'That lady who trapped me in the woods a little while ago. The one who hairdryers her bunions.' I furtively point to the woman with whom we're very soon to cross paths if we don't speed up and change course.

'DENNIS!' Beryl calls out to him, lagging behind off the lead. 'Mummy's going now. Mummy's saying bye-byes,' she says, walking off with a mock wave in the same way a mother would to a stubborn toddler.

Dennis cocks a leg, wees on an empty crisp packet, then gives chase to catch up.

'Go! Go! Go!' I tell Rachel. 'Or we'll be here all night.'

I feel bad for being anti-social but my pangs for a pasty will never be satiated if we get cornered by Beryl. Knowing her, she'll start talking about her flakey foot skin which'll put me off the flakey pastry with my name on it in the bakery.

When we leave the park through an exit at the top of some steps leading into town, I look back with relief. Her, Dennis and her bunion have gone off in the opposite direction. Dennis is sniffing the ground Pearl just soiled. He catches her scent and scans the park for her, ears aloft.

Not this time, Dennis, you randy little mutt. Go hump someone else's hound!

We make it to Greenhalgh's Bakery with five minutes to spare before closing time. I slip on my mask and go inside. Pearl and Rachel wait by the entrance outside.

'What have you got left?' I ask a lady behind the counter in a green overall and white hat.

'Only meat and potato, I'm afraid,' she says.

'Perfect! One of those then, please.'

She puts a pie on the top of the glass display case.

'Sorry. I actually wanted a pasty, if you've got any.'

'You said you wanted meat and potato.'

'Yeah. A pasty though, please.'

'If you want a meat and potato pasty, you have to actually say "meat and potato pasty,"' she educates me. 'If you just say "meat and potato," you'll get a pie.'

'Oh. I didn't know that,' I say. 'So, erm. Can I have a meat and potato pasty then, not a pie, please?'

'Poof,' she says.

Poof? Is she using outdated, unkind and completely politically incorrect language to suggest I have homosexual tendencies?

'Poof?' I balk.

'Poof pastry okay? We've got no plain left.'

'Oh. Erm. Yeah. Puff pastry's fine, thanks.'

Rachel, still standing in the doorway with Pearl, laughs at me.

'You haven't got any vegan pasties left by any chance, have you?' I enquire on Rachel's behalf.

'They're all gone, sorry, love. We've got cheese and onion pies int' fridge, though.'

I look at Rachel. She gives me the nod that this passes her vegetarian's test.

'Can you warm it up?' I ask.

'Of course.'

'Thanks!'

She places my meat and potato pasty from the window display on top of the counter. I get a cheese and onion pie from the fridge behind me and put it next to my pasty. Then there's an awkward few seconds of silence during which I expect her to whisk away Rachel's pie to warm it up. She doesn't.

'Thanks then, love,' she says.

'Can you warm up the pie then, please?' I remind her.

'No, but you can warm it up,' she says, pointing at me.

'I think we've got our wires crossed,' I say. 'I asked, can you warm it up and you said, of course.'

'Yes. You can warm it up,' she repeats. 'When you get home.'

'But I was actually asking if you, yourself, could warm it up. Here. Now?'

'No, we don't warm the pies up, I'm afraid.'

'But there's a microwave just there,' I say. 'Only takes two minutes.' I point to the heating instructions on the packet.

'I'm sorry, we don't do that,' she repeats, standing her ground.

I want to shout, 'This makes no sense at all! Warm up my wife's pie, right here and now, like you said you could.'

But instead, I just stand there, silent and confused.

'You're not from reauwnd 'ere, are you, love?' she says like it's more a personal disadvantage than a question.

Chapter 12

Royal Flush

Neighbours! Everybody needs good neighbours! Preferably neighbours that don't build a wall of horse manure around their property like the Murray family did in New Brunswick, Canada. They were successfully sued by their neighbours who demonstrated in court that the partition of poo was so large and stinky that it could be seen on Google Earth. A judge ordered the Murrays to pay $15,000 in compensation and recommended they "keep their shit to themselves!"

We consider ourselves very lucky that we haven't had to deal with such horseplay since we moved in. On one side, we have a young and very friendly couple with two kids. We often exchange neighbourly niceties when we bump into each other putting the bins out on Sunday nights.

'Load of rubbish this, int'it?' the lad next door joked the first time it happened.

Occasionally we get a knock on the front door from their little boy. He very politely asks if we can throw his football back over the back garden fence.

''Course I can!' I always tell him when I really want to say, 'Only if you stop wearing that Manure, I mean, Man U (Manchester United) shirt.'

On the other side we have a ghost. Someone we've still not seen since we moved in.

For the last three months, we've been passing ships with a character that exists only in my imagination. Someone that I'm assuming to be rather well-to-do. I've put this person on a pedestal because they do what all well-to-do folk do. And no, I don't mean they procure goods from Nowt In Sod All. This person shops at Sainsbury's. I know this because a van pulls up outside for a delivery every Wednesday.

Whilst walking Pearl at night, through their living room window I've spied lamps that look like mini, tabletop chandeliers, a beige, reclining luxury three-piece suite, and the upper-class productions they like to watch on television: *Homes Under the Hammer*; *Antiques Roadshow*; *Newsnight*. In our house, it's *Family Guy*, if on the odd occasion I get my way. Most of the time, though, it's Rachel watching dating shows, *Bake Off* or *RuPaul's Drag Race* during which I ask her confused questions like:

'Why does RuPaul call the drags squirrel friends?'

'Because they hide their nuts.'

Who knew?

I also assume our mystery neighbour is highbrow because they have various styles of hats hanging on a stand in their front porch and a stone statue of a white lion guarding their front door.

As you'd expect, they drive a vehicle of distinction and status. Behind the head-high golden gates of their driveway is a brand-spanking-new white Mercedes.

So . . . hats, statues, high-end cars and golden gates! We could be talking a celebrity here! Maybe royalty? And who'd have thought, next door to little old me?

They must be so pumped and loaded with cash that they've even got their own gardener, too. I've seen a man in a green fleece and grey combat pants in their back garden ripping up weeds, mowing and trimming their lawn, and pruning their bushes. Potted plants take pride of place on their patio. Providing the finishing touches to their luxury outdoor landscape, they have solar-powered fairy lights draped around an apple tree at the bottom of their garden that light up come sundown.

In the famous words of Lloyd Grossman on the TV show *Through the Keyhole*, "Who would live in a house like this?"

One prediction I can make is that a sole female occupant lives in a house like this. The washing line is a dead giveaway. I've spied green underwear and two knee-length dressing gowns hung out to dry, one pink and one duck-egg blue. I've also seen turquoise pyjamas with flying sheep on them swinging in the wind, and a white t-shirt emblazoned with the words "Girls Just Wanna Have Sun" in big, black print.

Further building the profile of this person, I was astounded to find out they have their own personal fisherman. A white van with "*Fresh from the sea, come and see Lee*" written in an italic font on the sides turns up on Friday mornings. A man who I'm assuming to be Lee, looking very fresh from the sea in a white overall and blue pinny, jumps out of the van carrying a polystyrene tray with frozen fish, rings the intercom, then enters the estate through the gates.

It's come to my attention that my neighbour turns in for the night around 11pm, when the vintage French draperies, or curtains as us ordinary people call them, in the upstairs bedroom are drawn. I know this because it's the time I take Pearl into the back garden to water the plants before Rachel and I hit the sack. Back inside soon after, upstairs, I often hear a bowel movement through the bedroom walls followed by a royal flush.

I do worry momentarily that by knowing all these very intimate, some might say, creepy details about someone I don't know, I might be turning into a stalker. Just to check my curiosity about my neighbour isn't in danger of spiralling out of control, I Google support groups but find nothing. I consider starting my own self-help group. It'd be called "Stalk and Talk" or "Hide and Speak."

In the end, I reason that I'm not a stalker, or on stakeout. Neither am I obsessed or a peeping Tom. I've just been trying to keep myself entertained during lockdown, and most days these have been the most interesting things going on. Oh, and a new speed camera sign was installed on the road running past our house. Life in the fast lane, I'm sure you'll agree. Hope, the lollipop lady, will be very happy.

Then one evening, December darkness already descended, there's a knock at the door.

My first thought is, Who the bloody hell is this? Don't they know I'm busy thinking up names for my drag alter ego? So far I've come up with Barack O-bummer, Whoopi Goldballs and Will Hung.

'Who is it?' Rachel shouts upstairs from the shower over "White Christmas" playing and the whooshing of running water.

'I don't know, I've not opened the door yet!'

Sarcasm really is not my greatest virtue. It's any wonder Rachel puts up with me.

Petulantly grumbling to myself about not having time for bloody carol singers while I'm trying to decide on my drag name, I unbolt the latch and poke my head around our front door.

'Ow's yer bog?' asks a wrinkled lady with grey roots sprouting in dyed, bleach-black, shoulder length hair.

'Sorry?'

'Your toilet? 'Ow's your toilet?' she asks again with big-hooped earrings swinging in a bitterly cold wind rushing in through the front door.

'Mine's not flushing proper-leh! I'm Maggie from't next door-wah, by the way.'

'Erm . . . Our water pressure can be a bit weak sometimes,' I report. 'Toilet's okay, though.'

'I've phoned me plumber,' she says, making a phone out of her little finger and thumb on her right hand.

'Ah, thanks,' I say, then wonder why I'm thanking her for phoning someone to look at her toilet.

Just as I'm about to ask if Sharon from A Mutt Above has been in her house and blocked her toilet with a Christmas log –

'Oops. 'Fore I forget,' she says, pointing at the floor, 'got you and your lady this for Christmas.'

I look down where there's a Marks & Spencer Christmas hamper in a basket packed with goodies – festive chutney; shortbread; a bottle of Claret Bordeaux.

'Wow! Thank you!' I say, feeling bad that we've not got her anything (Rachel would soon right that wrong by making her a cheesecake). 'You've even put in some dog treats. That's so kind of you.'

'You're welcome, lovey. I'm taking pee downstairs, now.'

See, I told you she was posh. Christmas hampers AND a downstairs toilet. Oh, how the other half live up here!

Chapter 13

Farewell So Long

Irish rockers U2 have a song called "Seconds" that goes a little something like, '. . . it takes a second to say goodbye, say goodbye, oh oh oh.'

From my experience, they take a lot longer than that in the north of England . . . A helluva lot longer.

Since our first Christmas after our move back home was spent all on our lonesome because both of Rachel's parents and her grandad contracted Covid (and thankfully fully recovered), I'm zooming right now back to happier times.

It's Boxing Day night, 2019, three months after Rachel and I tied the knot. We've come back home to Bolton from Tenerife to spend Christmas with Rachel's family. It's my first northern Christmas.

All the Lee family (Rachel's maiden name) are over at Grandad Stanley's. And when I say all the family, I mean every single last one of the clan. Even Bruce Lee has made an appearance and is karate chopping Christmas crackers instead of pulling them. Though there's not enough room to swing a cat, there's just enough room to fit in the five family dogs. As well as Pearl and Millie, who you've already met, Eric the Labrador is here barking for buffet scraps; Oscar the

West Highland Terrier is picking a fight with the letterbox flapping in the wind; and Max, the cocker spaniel puppy, is trying to mate with anything and everything in his sight to within an inch of its life. No one and nothing is being spared his primal urges. Him, Dennis and the crazy NISA shopkeeper would be dangerous were they to team up. More Randy Old Dogs than *Reservoir Dogs*.

To make sure everyone could get their bum on a seat, the family have brought bean bags, pouffes and stools over from their houses. When we realised that still wasn't enough seating once cousins, aunties, uncles and all their partners had squeezed into the living room, I dug out, cleaned up and tightened up the screws on some old rickety chairs from Stanley's garage.

Knowing full well the Lees are a devout, churchgoing Catholic family, I was expecting many a Christmas tradition to be upheld. I didn't know exactly what that would entail because I'm not a Catholic or a churchgoer, but I imagined we might break some bread, drink some wine and sing "Away in a Manger" by candlelight. Well, we didn't do any of that, but we did play 'Turd in the Hole.' This is a game in which you attach a hot dog to a piece of string, tie it around someone's waist, and then encourage them to squat until they're able to drop the hot dog into the hole in a toilet roll. Get the 'Turd in the Hole,' if you will. Stanley got the biggest cheer when he did so. We piled two loo rolls on top of each other so he didn't have to squat too low.

The Olympoop Games didn't stop there. We also played 'Poohead.' In this activity, someone assumes the role of target by strapping a Velcro toilet to their head. After that, contestants have to launch a big, brown Velcro Mr Whippy at the victim's toilet head from a distance in the hope it sticks. Each time the shit hit the head, the place erupted!

Come half past midnight, with time having flown while we've been having so much fun and laughter together, Rachel's mum, Maria, brings an official end to proceedings.

'Is it that time already?' she says, standing up from her chair at the back of the living room behind the buffet table. 'We best call it a night.'

This sets the valedictory domino in motion and everybody prepares to leave. People stand up. Trousers get pulled up. Knickers and pants get pulled out of arse cracks. Car keys start jingling. Phones get checked for notifications. Bruce Lee unties the black belt from around his waist to make space for all the food he's eaten from the buffet. Max the puppy is so excited by all the new activity that he goes to hump his toy teddy bear until it squeaks in ecstasy.

While all this is happening, I'm beginning to get increasingly nervous. This is a situation I've never been in before. I have to say goodbye to a room full of people that I hardly know but who are all now officially my family. I have no idea what the norm is for saying goodbye amongst my northern in-laws. Is a kiss on the cheek too much, too soon? A hug over the top? A handshake too formal? Walking away with just a wave from a safe distance and a "see you later" like I normally would, too cold? Too southern? Maybe I should just hug the women, but shake hands with the men? I somehow have to come up with a plan to find out how to say goodbye with my new family.

'I'll go defrost the windows in the hire car,' I whisper to Rachel.

How will this help me learn to say goodbye, I hear you ask? Well, I'll tell you, because this is genius. I'll be able to watch from inside the car how the first few folk exit the house, then I can return inside and follow suite. If they hug upon leaving, then I'll bring it in too. If they kiss, I'll pop in a Polo from the packet in the car door because I've had quite a few Scotch eggs from the buffet and my breath smells like Sharon the dog groomer's shit.

Doing as I said I would to Rachel, I fire up the heaters for the front and back windscreens, then turn on the radio. With the car idling and The Pogues' Christmas song "Fairytale in New York" playing on Smooth FM, I spray a can of de-icer over the back and front windscreens, all the while keeping a beady eye out for that front door to open and people to start leaving so I can watch and learn how my Boltonian brethren say goodbye.

After around five minutes waiting inside the car, that front door still hasn't opened, and not a soul has left. I try to look busy rather than suspicious in the driver's seat, and look up online if there is some kind of northern Christmas tradition for saying goodbye. Nothing comes up, but I do find a website with some interesting international customs. In some parts of India, when they wave someone off, they place a spoonful of lemon curd on the right hand of the person departing. In certain regions of Greece, mints are given. The Bedouins also have a tradition of placing one's nose on the other person's face and breathing in.

An idea pops into my head as "Last Christmas" by Wham! plays over the radio waves – why not take the initiative and start up my own tradition? I could give out some Polos just like the Greeks gifting mints. I could spoon a dollop of cheese and chive dip onto their hands from the buffet like the Indians do with lemon curd. Instead of sniffing facial skin and breathing in like the Bedouins, I could insist that we sniff each other's armpits. I could say it's what we do down south, the significance being that even though the person may soon be out of sight, they're not out of smell. Their essence forever getting up our noses. None of them would know any different, would they?

After 15 minutes sat in the car and still no one having left the house, I reluctantly accept that I'll have to go back inside before the neighbours suspect I'm up to something. I send Rachel a message and ask her to come let me in. She doesn't read it or reply.

'Thanks a bunch,' I complain to my phone screen. 'I let every single member of your family throw poo at my head and you can't even read my messages. Bloody charming!'

I ring the doorbell. Bruce Lee answers and lets me in with a bow. He then creaks the door closed using the power of his mind.

I re-enter the house ready to dish out the dips, mints and sniffs. I'm also mentally rehearsing farewells like 'Thanks for throwing shit at my head,' 'Congrats on getting the turd in the hole,' and 'Sorry about my Scotch egg breath.' I'm on alert to do whatever I need to say and do to get this over with.

It would appear, however, that no such words or actions are necessary because the big gathering that was seated around the perimeter of the living room and supposedly saying sayonara has splintered off into three separate groups.

There's now a gang in the kitchen talking about putting on a charity do for Bolton Hospice in the same church hall where Rachel's dad, DJ Disco Dave the Rave, volunteers and her mum helps out, too. Stanley's seven grandchildren have congregated around the telly where they are showing him how to tune in to Bolton Wanderers' YouTube channel. There's another gang of buffet slayers at the back of the room, picking at the picky tea and talking about Rachel's cousin's boyfriend's job as a fireman.

'In Manchester where I'm stationed,' Jack the lad says, 'they don't call it a ladder. They say ladd-or. "Get up the ladd-ooorrr!" they were screaming at me. I just stood there when I first started training. I didn't know what they were saying,' he says, shrugging his shoulders.

Now, I can't speak for everyone in the south of England. I can only draw from my own social experiences and those shared with close family and friends. But, when we say goodbye, we immediately skedaddle. We're out the door. We've done one. Baked potataaaaa! That's cockney rhyming slang for "see you later," by the way.

Up here in the north, more than a half hour since "We best be off," all are still in attendance with no signs of anyone skedaddling.

'I thought we were leaving.' I sidle up to Rachel, who's explaining a recipe for dog-friendly cupcakes to her cousin.

'We are,' she says. 'We're just saying goodbye.'

I survey the room where current activity doesn't appear to back up her statement. A new group has assembled around Stanley who's showing off his reissued bus pass because he'd lost his old one. Max is so excited by Stanley's free travel around the Greater Manchester area, he's grabbed hold of my left leg with his front paws and is launching his lance at my kneecaps. I exhale a cloud of Scotch egg breath at him to kill the moment of passion. Thankfully he recoils, tongue hanging out of mouth, then lets his teddy bear have it yet again.

Not knowing what to do with myself, I go back to the buffet where I can look busy eating Scotch eggs. I force-feed myself two more, then pop my head around the kitchen door to see what's going on. Rachel's dad is holding the baton of conversation. They're no longer talking about fundraisers.

'Whitney Houston, bisexual? You're joking!' he exclaims. 'When she said she wanted dance with somebody, I were 'oping that were me back int' 80s. I had no bloomin' chance, did I? She'd have danced with anybody,' he says, eyes closed, head back and chortling at his own joke. 'Least I've still got me Kylie Minogue.'

My eyes stray to the clock on the kitchen wall above the kettle. It's a full hour since we were saying goodbye. Then Rachel's dad, seeing me standing in the hallway listening, catches me unawares.

'I thought you said we were going,' he says.

'Eh?'

'We're waiting for you lot in there, start making tracks,' he says.

'I've had my coat on for the last hour ready to go,' I say. 'I thought we were leaving when Maria said so.'

'Are you winding me up?' he jokes. 'I've just poked me head around door and seen you lot in there mucking around ont' telly with me dad.'

'Not guilty on that one,' I plead. 'I've already been out to defrost the car.'

'Is that cockney rhyming slang for telling lies? Come on, you. Start rounding 'em up. You've gotta be ruthless in our family or we'll never get out of 'ere.'

I march into the living room ready to be ruthless, but new conversations have started and new groups have formed. Rachel's sibling cousins, Terri, Billy, Stacey and Leah are all sat on the sofa with their arms around each other's shoulders for a photo. Throughout the night, it became obvious they were all really close, and it was lovely to see how they looked out for each other. In the games we played, I noticed how the two more confident siblings would surreptitiously make it easier for their shyer, less confident siblings to succeed (making the toilet roll hole bigger for their "poos" when they weren't looking, for example) so they could get big cheers and a little boost of self-esteem from the crowded room. Although I didn't know it at the time, it was a glimpse of what we'd be returning home to just eight months later – a united family network who are there for us and each other.

I want to ask Rachel for help to start clearing the room, but she's slow-dancing with her grandad to Elvis Presley's "Can't Help Falling in Love" playing on YouTube. There's no way I can interrupt either Rachel or her cousins during such special moments. Instead, I get my phone out and film Rachel and Stanley slow-dancing so that we'll have the moment to look back on and treasure forever.

Unsuccessful in my bid to get the fat lady singing, I return to the buffet. I'm more nervous than ever now. Not only because I still don't know how to say goodbye, but also because I've got the added pressure my father-in-law has put on me to get people moving. The heating in the house on pizza oven settings isn't helping my anxiety either, because I've had my big coat on for more than an hour now and I'm beginning to sweat. As a coping strategy, I take my coat off and start chain-eating Scotch eggs, swallowing them whole one by one without chewing. Thankfully, just as I think I've had that many that I'm about to start clucking in a Scottish accent ("Back-kirk, ya wee fanny, back-kirk!" is how I imagine that might sound), Rachel's mum enters the fray and comes to the rescue.

'Come on, you lot,' Maria says. 'Let's be 'avin' yers or it'll be next Christmas 'fore you're all gone.'

'Who's clearing up picky tea?' asks Rachel's auntie.

'We'll do that int' morning,' says Rachel's mum. 'Don't worry.'

'No, you bloomin' won't. We'll do it together now,' Rachel's auntie insists. 'Won't take five minutes if we all muck in.'

While the mucking in begins gone 2am, 90-odd minutes since 'We best be off,' Rachel's grandad carries on a conversation with his grand-daughter, Terri, on the sofa.

'That's what you want, int'it?' he says. 'Fresh Warby's loaf int' morning for your toast. Ooooh.'

I make myself useful by putting chairs back where they came from, rounding up cups, plates and cutlery and hoovering up the last of the Scotch eggs with my mouth. Once the buffet table is cleared, Bruce Lee gives it a clean while quietly reciting the famous martial arts mantra, 'Wax on, wax off.'

'Bloomin' useless, you are,' Rachel's dad says, pulling my leg again as he stacks up the chairs to put back in the garage. 'I told you ages ago get rid of this lot.'

'You can talk,' I riposte. 'All you've done is stand around in the kitchen going on about Whitney Houston.'

Come half past two in the morning, some two hours since the night was first declared over, I hear the front door close.

'Has someone just gone?' I say to Rachel.

'Yeah. Annie and Abbie. They said to say goodbye because they didn't want to bother you while you were talking to Dad.'

Bugger! Two of Rachel's cousins have left, yet I'm still none the wiser or any calmer about saying goodbye. Rachel's mum, Maria, can't take anymore.

'Right, you lot,' she says, waving a pretend yet assertive fist at the partygoers. 'He's going working at half four int' morning and he's not even been bed,' she says, gesturing back over her shoulder at Rachel's dad.

For me, it's decision time. Do I hand out the Polos, smear people's hands in cheese and chive dip, or sniff some pits? Before I can make up my mind, I'm hugged, kissed, and having my hand shaken from all angles as the house starts to finally empty and cars drive off into the frosty Boxing Day night.

Just like I discovered the locals love a hello when I first arrived up north, I found out that night, that if my in-laws are anything to go by, they also love a very long and touchy feely goodbye.

Chapter 14

Storming It

'What's the biggest difference between people from the north of England and people from the south?' I quiz Google. In the search results, I find an internet forum with some highly amusing points of view.

"Northerners are straight talking whereas southerners are natural born liars. That's why most of them work in sales."

Did you know I've got another book for sale called *The Only Way Is West* about how I once walked 500 miles across Spain? If you buy one, I'll throw in a bookmark, a voucher for Nowt In Sod All, and Grandad Stanley's old clock. Bargain. Bosh!

"Northerners are friendlier and more outgoing."

Speaking from my early experiences up here, hard to argue with that one.

"Northerners wear t-shirts or skimpy dresses all year round, while southerners run off crying to the big coat shop as soon as August is over."

Guilty as charged! On the coats, not the dresses. The day after I arrived back in the UK late August, I asked Matalan to deliver unto me their warmest winter apparel. I'm actually wearing it inside the house now as I type.

"Northerners are generally rougher and tougher than soft southern shandy drinkers."

One weekend in January, I meet a man who would prove the keeper of that last thought very right.

On a wild and wet Saturday afternoon, we head out for a hike. It's chucking it down so hard that puddles are growing into ponds, streets are turning into streams, and the fields we drive past are fast becoming reservoirs.

With rain streaming down the windscreen severely blurring visibility of the road ahead, Rachel suggests we turn back. Go home. Put the telly and the heating on, then slip into our onesies that Rachel's mum bought us for Christmas. Rachel got a cow and I got a penguin. While that does sound very appealing, I refuse to be beaten. Motivated by those comments I read online, I want to prove the mocking northerners wrong. I want to show that us supposedly soft, shandy-drinking southerners can rough it with the best of them. I, we, can do this! Long as I've got my Matalan big coat on. Which, I do, of course.

I try bellowing some motivational words to Rachel as we start our walk in the rain- and wind-lashed woods, but it's so cold, and the muscles in my cheeks are so whipped and frozen by the icy windchill that I'm not able to finish the sentence.

'Makes you feel alive!' I try to shout. It sounds more like, "Mays oo fee ai."

I pull the cords of my big hood on my big coat a little tighter to keep the cold off my face so I can talk again and don't sound like I've had my mouth numbed by a dentist's injection.

Rachel, who's a few yards behind me with Pearl slaloming puddles, says something in reply but I can't quite hear her because pressure-washer rain is slapping the waterlogged ground. I can just about hear, however, very faintly on the path ahead, a whistle. Two notes. The first, a higher pitch than the second. I've heard this whistle before. It can only be Pete. Or, as he calls himself on Facebook, Pete the Birdman. He has a quote on his profile written under his name:

**"Birds' hearts beat to the rhythm of the music,
for theirs is the same religion as mine."**

The distinctive ditty that he uses to alert the birds that it's feeding time gets louder as we walk on.

I've seen Pete in here a few times before, crouched down on his haunches with the little tweetie pies eating seed out of his hands. Last time I bumped into him on a less rainy day, he insisted on stopping to show me a clip of a robin on his phone.

''Ere! Like me tap-dancing robin?' he said, then showed me a video of a robin hopping along the rails of a wooden footbridge inadvertently in time to a woodpecker drilling a tree trunk.

To find the recording of the tap-dancing robin, he had to swipe through endless photos he'd taken on his phone of different kinds of trains – steam trains, old trains, new trains, even toy trains. He had that many photos of trains, and seemed to like them so much, I thought he was going to ask me if I wanted to do the locomotion with him through the woods. Birds and trains. What a lovely life, eh?

Today, Pete is up ahead on the path with his two Jack Russells, Roy and George, named after his wife's favourite pop star, Boy George. They're fetching objects Pete is throwing, dropping them at his feet and then barking at him for more.

'We call it Game o' Cones,' Pete shouts over the rain, presenting a pine cone in his right hand.

'What d'ee say?' Rachel yells, pulling her hood aside to hear me better through the rain once we'd left them behind.

'He said they call it Game of Cones,' I say.

'Why?'

'Like *Game of Thrones*, I suppose.'

'I don't get it.'

'Like the TV series,' I enlighten her before turning around and walking into a naked branch protruding onto the path that nearly gouges my eyes out.

'Ohhhhhh,' she says, finally connecting the dots.

We trudge on through curtains of rain, splashing through sodden soil underfoot that's fast morphing into marshland. I make a mental note to bring my snorkel for next time.

When we come to a muddy and meaty incline, we slip and slide our way to the top, grabbing onto tree branches and thick roots to pull us up and keep our balance. At the apex, we take a moment to catch our breath.

'I saw on my Facebook memories today,' Rachel says, nestling her head between my chest and armpit to shield herself from the wind and rain, 'this time last year, we were having tapas on sun beds at the beach.'

'Don't remind me,' I sigh, looking up at the grey clouds leaking.

Pearl, who is normally shy and retiring, has an uncharacteristic outburst as she shakes rain off her coat. 'I was laying by your side on a cooling mat under a parasol and now look at me in this stupid fucking luminous orange fleece.'

I fear that Rachel, who abhors any form of swearing, is about to castigate her with no treats for a week. She doesn't.

She just says, 'Awww. I know this must be a big change from Tenerife for you, baba,' then strokes her head.

This is not fair. If I swear, I get told off and the silent treatment until I say sorry. Pearl gets pardoned and pat on the head. If I fart, I get told to leave the room and not come back until I've been to the toilet. Pearl gets an 'Awwww, she can't help it.'

I rue these double standards as, from the top of the hill, I assess how we'll get down the other side. The decline is less a path and more a mudslide. We'd have to skid down on our arses or stomachs like we're on a waterslide. Descending on foot is an impossibility.

We're left with no other option than to turn back, but I do so with peace of mind that we've taken this expedition as far as we can. I've shown that us southerners can get down and dirty with the northerners. That we don't all shirk or shy away at the first sign of meteorological adversity. I'm already thinking about rewarding myself with a shandy and a bigger coat.

About to turn around and carefully go back down the way we came that has trees we can grab onto and rocks and gravel to give us some traction, we run into a quite extraordinary individual that is coming up the hill.

The fact that he's wearing shorts on a stormy January day doesn't surprise me anymore and is no longer a novelty. He does appear, however, to be at a disadvantage that would keep most people at home in even the best weather, let alone a torrential downpour. While his right leg appears to be in fine fettle, his left appears to be severely restricted. It is, in fact, in a very muddy plaster cast.

I still can't quite comprehend what I'm seeing. I squint to make sure my eyes do not deceive me. They most certainly do not. This man has left the house to battle the biblical elements with one fully functioning leg. And two crutches!

He lifts a crutch and points ahead to the downhill section I just declared impassable.

''Ow bad is it?' he asks, getting his breath back.

'Very bad.' I puff out my cheeks (on my face, not my arse), raise both eyebrows and make my eyes bigger to emphasise just how bad it is.

'Is it really that bad?'

'Really, really bad. Like a mudslide.'

'I like mud,' shouts a little blond girl no older than five huffing and puffing as she gets to the top of the hill.

'Me too!' agrees a young boy running up the hill just behind her.

'Good girl, Princess,' shouts the old man, who I'm guessing is the little girl's grandad.

Then up come three more of his bouncing bloodline!

What a man! What a grandfather! What a maniac! One leg in plaster, yet still determined to take the grandkids for a hike in conditions the weather reporters would soon confirm is the opening act of Storm Christoph. Swathes of Northern England are in the early stages of being flooded by more than their average January rainfall in just two days.

'What you done?' I ask the gritty grandad.

'What, this?' he answers, looking at his bad leg. 'Just broke me th'ankle. I'll be reet,' he replies, playing it down. 'Let's 'ave a go, shall we?' He rallies the five grandkids, pointing towards Mudslide Hill.

'YEAH!!' they all scream.

And off they go, "'avin a go." I fear he'll have more than a broken "th'ankle" if he goes down that hill. We stop, watch and silently pray he doesn't break a th'arm, th'leg or his th'back, too.

The man lurches towards the decline, dragging along his bad leg and his five grandkids who are now throwing mud at each other.

'Shall I go help him?' I ask Rachel.

'You can't, baba,' Rachel says. 'You mustn't get too close 'cos of Covid.' She's right. I couldn't, shouldn't help him even if I wanted to.

With a crutch pointing the way, he signals to the kids to follow him down. They do. Once they're out of sight, and all has gone quiet, Rachel and I poke our heads over the top of the hill. We're expecting to see them all strewn about the hillside on their backsides covered in mud. But they're not. They've done more than "'ave a go." They're already down at the bottom and Grandad is now leading the mud-fighting kids back off into the woods.

A few hours later in the warmth of our living room in my penguin onesie, I realise I've still got a lot of toughening up to do if I want to rough it like the locals.

While Rachel laughs at Ivana Kutchakokoff, on *RuPaul's Drag Race* on the box, I fizz open a can of shandy and reflect that next time I think I can't do something, I should at least "'ave a go." As that gritty grandad proved, there's often a way to get something done, even when it may appear there's no way.

Chapter 15

Fe-bra-rary

I magine you're a contestant on the northern version of *Who Wants to Be a Millionaire?* It's called *Who Wants to Win a Million Buttered Butties?*

The final question to bank the grand prize and a lifetime's supply of lubricated loaves is . . .

> "What is the longest man-made waterway in the United Kingdom of Great Britain?"

The options are:

A. The Worcester and Birmingham Canal

B. The River Thames

C. The Leeds and Liverpool Canal

D. The Kennet and Avon Canal

If you'd have phoned a friend and they advised options A, B or D, you may well now count them as enemies.

The correct answer then, as I'm sure the Sherlocks among you have deduced by now, is the Leeds and Liverpool Canal.

And, by a gracious stroke of Lady Luck, I find myself living but a short seventeen-minute drive away from this magnificent feat of engineering carved into the northern English countryside during the industrial age.

Construction of the canal began in 1770. Its main purpose was to supply traders at Liverpool's international docks with an affordable supply of coal from Yorkshire's myriad mines. More than a million tonnes per year were transported northwest during the canal's heyday in the 1860s. The coal was in high demand on Merseyside to help drive its booming shipping and manufacturing businesses.

Spanning the width of Northern England, the waterway is 127 miles long and traverses the Pennines, Yorkshire Dales and Lancashire Moors. It's a veritable hidden gem.

The building of the canal took almost 50 years to complete, and though nowadays it's used more by ducks going for a dip than for dealing coal, its waters are still flowing strong today.

With Rachel on a half-term break from school and my online teaching duties done for the day, we set off mid-afternoon to explore the canal. We're delighted to find some bustling local life where people are enjoying their "outdoor exercise" privileges during the latest lockdown. Families are strolling. Runners are puffing. Power walkers – or as my mum calls them, wiggly walkers – are walking and talking (shout out to my mad mother there). Cyclists are grinding their gears and ringing their bells from behind to get past. Canoeists are splashing through the water with their oars. Narrow boats are humming along as they coast at the canal's speed limit of 5mph. Rachel, as always, is snapping photos every few seconds, desperate not to miss a moment.

High up in pewter skies, black flecks of flocks of birds are performing fly-bys like planes in an air show. Bare branches on the trees overhanging the murky canal on both sides are quivering in the cold.

Quacking ducks are carving triangular patterns in the water behind them as they glide gracefully downstream. Gangs of geese in the fields abutting the water heckle the ducks with incessant honking as they paddle by. A group of birdwatchers on one side of the canal are crouched down and huddled together, marvelling at a kingfisher amongst the reeds on the other. One birdwatcher has binoculars resting on his belly and an eye trained on the lesser-spotted avian through a camera lens as long as a sniper's rifle. There's a procession of fellow dog walkers, too. One of them hangs me out to dry with his quick northern wit.

'He looks like a mini Rottweiler,' I say, tentatively stroking his best friend when he boisterously jumps up at me and nips at my fingers.

'You'd be right,' he replies. 'He's Rottweiler puppy.'

'Really?' I squeal in hitched-pitched panic, pulling my hand away before its torn off.

'No, course not,' the man laughs. 'Just 'avin you on. He's a little Lancashire Heeler, really.'

'Good one!' I say, trying and failing to hide my red-faced embarrassment.

The man walks off chuckling to himself, commanding that his excitable heeler heel. Rachel laughs at me. Pearl has already trotted off, hoping none of her canine companions have seen or heard. She looks back over her shoulder and shoots me a despairing look that says, 'I'm not with you.'

Soon after, a little boy in a Manchester City tracksuit stops in his tracks in front of us, lies on his belly by the canal side, reaches into the water lapping the banks, and grabs a mucky tennis ball bobbing up and down.

'Do you want this for your dog?' he kindly offers, holding up the dripping ball.

'I'm alright, thanks, mate. You keep it. Do some skills.'

'Thanks!' he says, then tries and fails to bounce the sodden ball. It thuds into the ground and sticks into the mud.

Continuing on our way, I ponder how enchanting interactions like these ones with the young lad and the dog walker are really helping me settle in and feel at home. Unlike where I lived down south, the locals up here tend to see strangers as friends, not threats. It's so endearing. The natives of the north seem generally more approachable. They're entertaining; unapologetically authentic; bursting with character, life and wit. They're loaded with memorable one-liners and quick come-backs like they're reading from a sitcom script. Despite the rotten weather, I have a comforting thought that life up north is growing on me.

As a lady waters some plants on the top of her moored barge, I get a warm, fuzzy feeling in my heart. Not only do I like life up north, I'm actually beginning to love it.

Nearly as much as a long queue of people must love what they're waiting for, in the cold, at a kiosk up ahead by the canal side.

'I wonder what they're selling?' Rachel says.

'Tomato soup and bread, hopefully. I'd kill for something hot to warm me cockles,' I fantasise, rubbing my icy hands together to warm them up.

My wish is sadly not commanded. Turns out, they're selling something quite the opposite of hot: ice cream – Frederick's Ice Cream, nonetheless. As Bunion Beryl would say, it's all the range around these parts, even in big coat weather.

Had the queue for Frederick's not been so big and the risk of catching a cold from stopping to wait in the long line so high, we may well have tried some.

'Maybe next time,' we agree and saunter on.

The sun now has half a hat on. It's thinking about coming out, prising the odd shaft of light through the dense grey clouds but then taking its hat back off again. Maybe it's embarrassed that it hasn't shown its face around here in a very long time? I know I would be if I'd deserted my people when they needed me most during a winter in which thermometers plummeted to minus 21. Truth be told, after the UK's coldest winter in 26 years and unwelcome visits from Storm Christoph and the Beast from the East II, any sign of sunshine was more than welcome and felt long overdue. Like a surprise visit from a favourite friend you've not seen or heard from in a very long time.

Carrying on our way, taking in a colourful array of moored narrow-boats, granite stone waterside houses and beautiful arching bridges reflecting 3D images into the water, I pinch myself. I can't believe how lucky we are to live so close to somewhere so idyllic.

'Did you know?' I say, stopping to read from the Canal Trust website on my phone. 'From right here, we can walk to the Wigan Pier, Leeds City Centre and,' I pause for dramatic effect, 'Liverpool's Royal Albert Dock.'

'Can you pop this spot on me nose?' Rachel replies.

'Eh?'

'This spot,' she repeats, pushing on a flashing red blotch on the end of her nose. 'Can you pop it for me?'

'Errrr! No way. Pop it yourself.'

'My dad pops my mum's spots. And she wipes his bum.'

'What?'

'He had sciatica a few weeks ago and she had to wipe his bum 'cos he couldn't do it.'

'I don't want to know what you northerners get up to behind closed doors. We might not say hello down south, but at least we wipe our own arses.'

'Don't be daft. Come on, if my mum and dad can do that for each other, you should be able to pop my spot.'

'I did wipe someone's bum once when I volunteered at a care home. So I guess I could wipe yours,' I reason.

'In sickness and in health,' Rachel reminds me.

Caving in to her emotional blackmail, I do it there and then. Pop her spot (not wipe her bum) in broad daylight on the canal. That's right, with my two index fingers, I wince, then squeeze the yellow head on Rachel's nose flashing at me. Rachel thanks me, then hands me some disinfectant gel from her bag to clean my hands.

This, my friends, is real love, and my musings about the touristic jewels studding the canal path are forgotten for now due to spot popping duties.

Further downstream, as Rachel blots the spot with some tissue, some music in the middle distance makes our ears prick up. Very loud music. Dance music! Sounds like someone, somewhere, is having a party. Wherever this party is going on, we're getting closer to it.

Before long, on the other side of the canal, we spot a group of six women in jeans and wellies, throwing their arms around to some club hits blasting out of a portable Bluetooth speaker that they're pulling along a country lane on wheels.

I know it shouldn't surprise me after all the pale flesh I've seen on show in my first northern winter, but standing before us is another arresting sight. One of the ladies is so happy some sunlight has burnt through the fleecy clouds that she's thrown off a few layers of clothing, is half-naked and is bopping along to the music in a blue bra. A bouncing blue bra that's so big it looks more like a hammock.

'Shall I shout back to the birdwatchers that we've found some blue tits?' I joke to Rachel.

'I did say it's a bit nippy,' Rachel replies.

'Maybe,' I say, 'she's just nipped out?'

I start to get carried away with the puns now . . .

'Maybe, that's why they call it Fe-BRA-rary?' I giggle as Blue Tits trips over her wellies. She just about manages to keep her balance but spills half a can of the beer that she's drinking into the long grass tickling her knees.

This half-cut, half-naked lady gets me thinking about what's to come as the year warms up and the seasons change. If the men think nothing of slipping on a pair of shorts in sub-zero temperatures and women strip down to their bras in winter, what the hell is going to happen come the height of summer? Does the whole of the north of England turn into a nudist colony? Will my neighbour Maggie be doing the gardening with her growler out? Will my in-laws invite us over for barbecues in our birthday suits? I know they're my family now, but I'm still not sure I know them well enough to show them my cockney conkers.

Seeing Blue Tits having the time of her life and this whole new happy world thriving down by the canal does, however, give me a bright idea.

'Let's do the lot!' I say to Rachel as a hippy couple wave to us from the helm of a red narrowboat spluttering past.

'The lot of what?' Rachel says, waving back to the couple.

'The canal,' I say, waving too. 'Let's walk from Leeds to Liverpool.'

'Really?'

'Really.'

To be continued . . .

Chapter 16

Clubbing

Studies have shown that belonging to some kind of club, movement or society can work wonders for your mental health.

Unless you join a Flower Trampling Club, then I imagine it'd have quite the opposite effect and you might want to seek professional help. Therapeutic help, I mean, not help to trample on flowers.

The kinds of clubs I'm talking about are real-life collectives like the Pylon Appreciation Society, who were formed by and for "people inspired by transmission towers." You can even nominate and vote for your Pylon of the Month if that gets your bits buzzing.

Perhaps you'd be more into the Roundabout Appreciation Society (UKRAS) who gather to "discuss their architecture, design and safety features." If that sounds like it would drive you round the bend, you might like to try the Extreme Ironing Club, who "combine the thrills of extreme activities, with the satisfaction of a well-pressed shirt." Their members have been filmed ironing in the central reservations of motorways, whilst skydiving and swimming with sharks. Both deranged and daring in equal measure!

After moving to a new place where I know no one apart from Rachel's family and friends, I too feel it's time I joined a club. Made some new friends of my own. Found a kindred spirit I can push in a bush when they're not expecting it. Someone I can slap on the shoulder and point at when they make me laugh.

In short, after that brutal Spanish lockdown and enduring two more since arriving home, I miss real life. I miss being human, feeling human and connecting with humans. Doing so via screens is a lousy, overrated substitute. It's high time I stop being a hermit and run with the human race again.

Looking for that spike in my happiness hormones now that the latest lockdown has been lifted, I'm on the lookout for clubs, societies or groups I could get involved with.

Whilst bagging up a Warby's loaf on a quick shopping trip for Grandad Stanley at the checkout in my locals Sainsbury's, a poster pinned to a chalkboard jumps off the wall at me.

George Formby Appreciation Society

We meet on the last Wednesday of every month (except December). No need to be able to play the ukulele but if you do, you'll have the chance to do so, or perhaps learn. So why not come along and help keep George's name alive whilst enjoying a convivial evening of friendship?

Isn't that just bloody lovely? A club celebrating the life and career of the late local musician most famous for the song "*When I'm Cleaning Windows.*"

I put it on the maybe list.

On the internet later on, I find a local club who've named themselves "MAD." This sounds about right for many of the people I've met so far in my time up here – the granny-humping shopkeeper; Bunion Beryl; Barry who burns holes in his swimming trunks; the man I saw wearing shorts, vest and flip flops walking in a winter wonderland; the gritty grandad battling storms and hills head-on with one leg; Blue Tits on the canal in Fe-bra-rary; our lollipop lady, Hope, who wants to twat drivers who don't stop around the head with her lollipop. They're all the good kind of MAD and should be members if they're not already

Clicking on their website, I'm disappointed to find out MAD. doesn't stand for Manchester's Absolutely Doolally Club as I was hoping. It actually stands for the Manchester and District Walkers Club. Although this sounds delightful, too, it's not quite what I'm looking for.

In the end, I respond to a post from a football team on Facebook that says:

Assistant Manager needed. Must be available Wednesday evenings and Saturday afternoons. PM or call Brett on 07*** ******

Though I hung up my football boots in my mid-twenties because I was having to limp around on stage on Saturday nights after being kicked around a football pitch just hours earlier, I still think I could be useful as a manager's assistant. Heck, I'd do anything a bunch of lads or lasses might need: halftime orange peeler; lace do-er upper; ball washer (actual round footballs, not hairy men's). I'd even don an overall, blue rinse my hair, stick in some curlers, be a tea lady and push a trolley around. I just need to feel part of something again. To contribute.

I get straight on the phone.

'Hello?'

'Is that Brett?' I check.

'Bloody hope so. Either that, or he's been kidnapped.'

I like him already.

'Who's this?' he asks.

'Brett, my name's Brad. I'm calling about the assistant manager's job.'

'You know it's f'football team, not assistant manager of Facebook?'

'Haha. Yeah, I gathered that.'

'You might 'ave, but some other joker didn't. He thought he were applying for job wit' Facebook.'

'You do get 'em, don't you?'

'Certainly do . . . Says 'ere you're calling from't Spain?' Brett says, curiously inflecting the end of the sentence.

'Yeah, that's right, I've not long moved here from Spain.'

'Are you mad?'

'Haha! No, but I did marry a Boltonian.'

'You are mad then! Can you come along this Wednesday night f'training?'

'Sure!'

'It's eight while nine,' he informs me in what sounds like dialect from the Yorkshire town of Barnsley.

'Eight o'clock until nine. I can do that!' I confirm.

'We'll see 'ow you get on . . .'

Brett's accent reminds me of a stint I once had coaching football in America with a lad from Barnsley. In a North Carolina bar, a territorial native took exception to our "limey asshole" presence.

'What are ya'll staring at?' the yokel growled at us, trying to incite a fight.

'Don't know, I've not got me animal book with me,' Lee, the lad from Barnsley, replied.

The aggressive yokel was so nonplussed by this dry-witted comeback that he just walked away shaking his head. It's a hilarious memory that's tickled me ever since whenever my memory is jogged.

When Wednesday evening football training comes, it's far from a good start. Not knowing the roads too well and being held up by roadworks, I arrive a full 15 minutes late.

The team of lads are already charging about the floodlit astroturf pitch, caged in by red, wire mesh perimeter fencing. The squad, half of them wearing green bibs, is made up of a mixture of men of varying ethnicities, ages, body shapes, heights and hair colours. There's two gingers, a few silver foxes and a couple of gents whose hairless heads are reflecting the floodlights.

'Time you call this?' Mocks Brett, tapping his wrist. 'We're goin' 'ome soon.'

'Sorry! I got lost, then the traffic piled up at some poxy temporary lights.'

'You not got satnavs "dan saff"?' he jibes, making fun of my accent.

'I thought I knew the way.'

'Riiight,' he says, tossing a ball back to one of the lads looking to launch a quick throw-in.

'We've lost two balls already over't fence. Couldn't hit the floor if they fell over this shower. Do you mind fetchin' 'em?'

''Course not.'

'They went over't there,' he says, pointing to an inhospitable wasteland of bushes, weeds and nettles behind one of the goals.

As requested and eager to please, I set off in search of the two missing footballs. It wasn't what I had in mind when I thought about being part of something, but I need to prove my value to my potential new team. If they've lost two balls, I shall find three! I must endeavour to overdeliver! As all the motivational gurus preach – always do more than asked and expected if you want to make a good first impression.

As I wade my way into the dense wasteland behind the goal, I try to get Brett's attention in an appeal for assistance. I throw open my arms to show him I don't know where to start. He waves a casual hand in my general direction. I nod to show I've got the unhelpful message but don't dare complain that I need more specific information to find the lost balls. I don't want to come across as awkward or argumentative. I want to showcase that I'm someone who's capable of taking the initiative. That I can work with what he's given me.

Upon taking a few more tentative steps into the waist-high no-man's-land, the hairs of some stinging nettles claw at my left calf, causing me to stumble into some thorns that pierce my skin and sink into my shin bones.

'Ahhhh!' I scream like I've gone outside in December without my big coat.

'You okay there?' Shouts Brett from the halfway line of the astro-turf.

'Think so! Just some nettles and thorns,' I shout back through gritted teeth.

'You're not from reauwnd 'ere, are you?' asks the goalkeeper with a bulging belly in the goal just a few yards away on the other side of the perimeter fencing.

'Essex boy,' I give my standard reply to what's becoming a standard question. 'How can you tell?'

'Crying about nettles like southern pansy,' he says. 'Dead giveaway.'

'They don't 'alf bloody sting,' I complain, itching my legs. 'Did you see where the balls went?'

'One over't there,' he says, pointing diagonally right. 'T'other over't there.' He points diagonally left before turning around to see the ball fly past him into the goal.

'Thanks a lot, pal. Look what you made me do,' he grumbles, picking the ball out the back of the net.

This is going from bad to worse. First I'm late, then I yelp like a "southern pansy" because I get stung by a nettle and clawed by some thorns, then I make the keeper let in a goal. I'm not endearing myself to my potential new teammates.

As I continue my search, someone heckles me from the passenger seat of a souped-up black hatchback.

'WANKER!' they shout as it explodes through the gears and races off up the road running adjacent.

'Knows you well, does he?' the goalie chuckles to himself.

'Not my day this, is it?'

This is becoming more embarrassing by the minute.

Hunting high and low, I don't find the footballs, but I do find the skeleton of a bulky 90s television, a large chunk of a car bumper, the carcass and blood-stained feathers of a dead pigeon and, quite disturbingly, what looks like a chunk of a weather-beaten gravestone. Maybe they perished looking for lost footballs? It's not a good omen.

'Bastard!' I blurt out as some nettles taser me again.

'That's a bit harsh, we've only just met,' the goalie, ever the joker, comments over his shoulder while this time keeping a closer eye on the game. 'Any luck?' he asks.

'Not yet. What colour are they?'

'Yellow wit' Premier League logo,' he answers, pulling his green jersey down over his pasty paunch.

With 45 minutes of the hour training session gone and still no sign of the footballs, I wonder what I should do next. If I spend the whole time here, I won't be able to show off what I have to offer. I'd like to contribute to the team talks, put up some motivational quotes about the place, run up and down the touchline kicking every ball with them so that they feel like I'm their twelfth man. But if I abandon the search early, they might think I'm lazy, stupid or give up too easily. What example would that be setting if they make me part of the management team?

'I'll come back and look again afterwards,' I shout to the keeper.

'Okay-dokey.'

'No luck?' asks Brett when I return to the halfway line.

'None at all. Needle in a haystack over there.'

'Thanks for trying.'

'S'alright. I'll look again at the end,' I say.

With five minutes left, Brett claps his hands together to call the team over. The players gather in the centre circle.

'Lads, this is Brad. Brad, this is lads,' Brett announces. 'Brad's coming helping wit' games and training.'

'You not feauwnd them footballs, yet?' sniggers a stocky ginger lad with a mischievous, I-know-something-you-don't-know smirk.

'Not yet. I'll have another loo –'

Before I can finish my sentence, the entire team erupts into a chorus of laughter. Stiff shoulders start to shake. Straight faces crack, crease and crumple into guilty grins. Some point at me with their sides splitting as if to say, "We got you." Others double over, hands on their tickled ribs.

'That'll teach you be late,' Brett says. 'Welcome t' madhouse!'

Chapter 17

Pie Witness

Early morning, I witness a van recklessly reversing out of a dead end lane onto a blind bend. It's critically hidden by a line of thick conifers from the view of a car coming around the very same blind bend. It's the proverbial accident waiting to happen.

As a reluctant pedestrian bystander watching on in helpless horror from the pavement, I want to scream to the car driver that he should slam on the brakes because he's on a collision course for the reversing van, but he's got his windows up, music blaring and wouldn't hear my warnings. I want to shout to the van driver that a car is seconds away from piling into his vehicle, but he's still staring straight ahead when he should be looking in his mirrors or checking over his shoulder where he'd see me on the pavement leaking nervous wee.

Ten minutes prior, I could never have imagined I'd find myself in such a nightmare scenario of incontinence. I woke up to a stunning, sunny spring morning that I'd been longing for every day of a punishing winter. For the first time in a very long time, the sun radiated some welcome warmth in a dreamy, cloudless sky as I took Pearl out to cock a leg.

'Thank God, I don't have to wear that silly orange fleece anymore,' Pearl said, sniffing at a wet patch on a wall.

'Don't let your mum hear you say that,' I advised her, knowing how much the fleece means to Rachel because she spent seven quid on it in Home Bargains.

The bright morning rays sequinned every blade of dew-drenched grass on the front lawns in my neighbourhood. Like the graceful hands of a harpist, a gentle breeze caressed a wind chime hanging on a tree in someone's front garden into a pretty song. The smell of bacon sizzling in a bungalow kitchen escaped onto the street, whetting my appetite for breakfast. A district nurse playing "Back for Good" by Take That in her car with the window down wished me a good morning from the driver's seat as she carefully placed a Covid visor on her forehead in preparation for a house visit. An old man on a bike with thick, slicked-back grey hair pedalled by and did the same with a big, sincere smile.

'Ow do?' he said, pinching at his squeaky brakes while negotiating the handlebars around a corner.

I returned both of their greetings and went on my way, reflecting yet again on how friendly people are around here. For a moment I thought I'd moved to Pleasantville. Little did I know, things were about to turn very unpleasant.

Proudly swinging Pearl's perfumed and loaded poop bag like a school caretaker with a set of keys to show the neighbourhood that I'm a good dog owner, an amusing sticker in the back window of a rusting Ford Focus caught my eye:

NO PIES KEPT IN THIS VEHICLE
OVERNIGHT

This brought back memories of a night in Tenerife when a man from Wigan jumped on stage with me and pulled his top up to reveal a huge tattoo of a pie on his protruding belly. Written across his sagging chest, he had another tattoo:

CHIPPY TITS

Turning down a public bridleway and cutting through a cow field, some the wiser about where I shouldn't be looking to thieve pies if I ever wanted to, a muscly, green-pike-flecked-with-white sheep hoved into view to my right. To my left, beyond miles of flat open fields, hedges and electricity pylons that would turn on the members of the Pylon Appreciation Society, a hazy and distant view of Manchester – church spires poking over tree tops on the outskirts; a cluster of factory chimneys billowing smoke; modern skyscrapers dominating the skyline in the city centre, their windows reflecting the rays of the rising sun.

All was still quiet as I followed the bridleway alongside a plush primary school field where a lone magpie pecked at a crisp packet in the grass. One for sorrow. Another win, perhaps, for the superstitious, given the sorry scenario that awaited quite literally just around the corner.

Striding back onto the residential streets from the country lanes, that's when I hear it – the hitched-pitched rev of the van engine in reverse that'll haunt me forever.

Accelerating backwards out of the conifer-lined dead end, the van man is handling his vehicle like a getaway driver. The man at the wheel in the car, tapping the steering wheel in time to his music, is none the wiser that he's just a few revolutions of his wheels away from careening into the van.

What if the van driver has actually committed a crime? There's some fancy houses around here that he could have just ransacked. He could be fully loaded with stolen pies for all I know.

I fear that I'm now a potential witness that could put him behind bars. Will it be a hit and run and kill me too as the only person who could put him behind bars? All manner of scary scenarios bounce around in my brain as I freeze on the spot, tense up and instinctively look the other way, not wanting to see something that could scar me for life.

Gritting my teeth and squeezing my eyes shut, I hear a vehicle screech to an emergency stop. Then another quicker, shorter, quieter skid of the tyres. The smell of burning rubber diffuses. I hear a door click open and both engines idling, the diesel engine of the van more prominent than the car's. Only then do I dare to turn around and survey the damage.

There's no broken glass on the road. No blood spattered on windscreens. No dents. No bumpers hanging off. No crumpled bonnets. No airbags inflated. Neither are there any stolen pies spilled all over the road. Both vehicles are miraculously intact. I hope both drivers are, too.

Even though a collision has been avoided, anxious thoughts soon kick in about what's going to happen next between the drivers. Are they going to play the blame game that escalates into an ugly episode of road rage?

Two recent studies have uncovered that the UK has the second worst road rage rate in the world (after South Africa) and that four out of five Britons have been victims of road rage. These stats don't bode well with the trouble brewing.

There is an uneasy and fragile moment of calm before the man in the grey Transit van reverses a few more yards to get a view of what all the screeching was about and why he's had to slam on the brakes. He draws up to the kerb, whirs down a window, leans out of it and cranes his neck. The guy is a unit. Looks like a prison guard. One of his biceps is the size of both my thighs. He's completely bald with tattoos on the side of his skull. Stubble. Head the size of a pumpkin. Forty-ish, I'd say. But never to his face. If I met him, I'd ask, 'What moisturiser do you use? You're positively glowing, sister!'

On the dashboard of his van is another sure sign that the van man could be a very dangerous character – a pink teddy bear holding a heart cushion that says, "I love my mum." Not really, I made that last bit up. It actually says, "I suck my thumb." I made that bit up, too.

What is true, however, is that both men are now out of their vehicles, looking each other up and down. It's surely only a matter of time until a war of words breaks out, with warnings to look where they're going, to be more careful and accusations of driving like Stevie Wonder after 10 pints.

As I make myself scarce to stay out of harm's way, I carefully listen out to see how the scene unfolds. The car driver, a tall and skinny young man in a black Nike tracksuit, breaks the silence.

'You shoulda carried on,' jokes the young lad. 'I could've 'ad day off work.'

'You okay, pal?' the van driver checks, sounding sincerely concerned.

'Yeah. Fine. Nightmare bend that, int'it?'

I walk home with my memory jogged of a similar near miss I saw when I was strolling through London once upon a time. An aggressive van driver, after nearly hitting a cyclist, got out and spat, 'Get off the road, you fackin' mug. What ja fink this is, fackin' Amsterdam?'

I also consider what my own response might've been. I have to admit, it would've been reeking of sanctimony, indignation and condescension. A moral obligation to teach the van man a lesson that a simple three point turn would've saved both motorists from that very close shave and me having to change into some wee-free underpants when I got home.

That wise young man, however, reminded me of a more valuable lesson: humour is the best medicine for (almost) everything. And of course, not to square up to men twice my size.

Chapter 18

Coin Tosser

'We've got no potatoes in for tea,' I yell to Rachel from behind the pantry door early one Sunday evening.

'Can't hear you! Where are you?' Rachel shouts, stepping back inside from the garden.

'Where we keep our pants,' I say, popping my head around the door. 'The pantry.'

'Very funny.' She eye rolls. 'What did you say?'

'I said, we've got no potatoes in for tea.'

'Said no southerner ever.'

'Eh?'

'You just called dinner "tea,"' she says, dropping the washing basket to the kitchen floor in great amusement. 'You're turning into a northerner.'

'Oh shit. I did, didn't I? What are you lot doing to me?'

It's the first time in my life I've called the final meal of the day, known by us southerners as dinner, "tea." Whatever next? Will I go for a walk along the canal wearing only a blue bra up top? Stride into a stranger's house, take a shit and stink it out a la Sharon, then go find Bunion Beryl and tell her all about my ailments?

'I once had a haemorrhoid,' I'll say to her. 'Felt like I was sitting on a squash ball every time my arse kissed a chair.'

The fact that the local dialect has crept into my consciousness is worrying, but I'll have to deal with this issue later. There's a more pressing matter at hand – Rachel's mum and dad are coming over this evening for dinner. Tea. Some scran. Whatever you want to call it.

We've invited them over to thank them for all they do for us. Silly little things that mean the world, like texting to ask if we need anything when they go shopping; looking after Pearl whenever we need a dog sitter; driving Rachel to and from work when her car had to go in for repairs. We want to show our appreciation to them for always being there. Living abroad where we had no one, we know more than most how much this kind of support means, and will never take it for granted.

Rachel told me earlier in the week during an ad break while she was watching *RuPaul's Drag Race* that she was going to rustle up a famous Lancashire dish called Potato Hash.

'Sound like a way to get high on carbs,' I said.

'Don't be silly. My nana Lyons (her mum's late mum) used to make it all the time,' Rachel set me straight. 'She said it was popular during the war to make the most of the rations. "Tattie 'Ash," she used call it. All you do is cook a load of onions, carrots, beef stock, minced beef and potatoes together in a big pan.'

'Don't fuck it up!' RuPaul warned her drags on the telly as they're about to perform now that the ads are over.

'I think he's talking to you,' I said to Rachel.

With us being caught short yet again of a vital ingredient on a Sunday evening, just like when we needed eggs for Stanley's birthday cake, this can mean only one thing – another trip to the Nowt In

Sod All – NISA supermarket. Another encounter with the mad, bad, granny-humping shopkeeper on the dark side of town looms.

Rachel asks if I need her to come with me, but I'm not sure she's ready to see old ladies getting thrusted at from behind through gritted, growling teeth like I did on my last visit.

'You crack on with chopping the veggies,' I suggest. 'I'll peel and cut up the potatoes when I come back.'

While Rachel gets prepping the onions and carrots, I hop in the car and take a deep, bracing breath. I'm hoping and praying my visit doesn't coincide again with that of a grandma's. I don't want to awaken with a jolt at 3am afterwards like I did last time. In my nightmares, the shopkeeper was lying across his counter wearing only Barry's crotchless swimming trunks and being fed Maltesers like grapes by bikini-clad grannies who were offering free scratch cards, but there was a catch – you had to go down their panties to get them. They were called "Snatch Cards."

'Lucky Dip?' one of the grannies offered, coquettishly pointing south at her landing gear in my nightmare.

Just as I did a few months back, I drive down that same long street of derelict, red-brick terraced houses on both sides, many of them in various states of neglect – long, uncut grass; wooden panels instead of windows; in front gardens, skeletons of rusting trampolines and wheelless bicycle frames. On the wall of a kid's playground, some fresh graffiti has been sprayed on the black background in enormous white letters:

I FARTED IN YOGA!

Next to it is a giant white stick man with a big smile cocking a leg in the air to break wind. I wonder if Banksy, Britain's anonymous, anti-authoritarian street artist, will come out and claim this one?

I pull over outside the shop and check around to make sure there's no shady characters around like there was the first time I came here. All seems quiet outside. Inside, it's another story.

Adopting my new anti-Covid way of entering a premise so I don't catch it from touching the handle, I nudge open the door with my elbow, then push it all the way back using my arse.

'Hello again, West Ham!' the shopkeeper says, recognising me. 'Are you wanting more eggs?'

Not only has he remembered my football team, but also what I bought on my first and last visit months ago. You don't get this kind of personal touch and shopkeeping-ship in Aldi.

'Potatoes, please!' I say.

'Up the back!' he says, throwing an arm towards the rear of the store.

I hope that's not what he says to the grannies, too!

As directed, I make my way to the back of the shop, listening out for any sneaky steps just in case he's crept up behind me and is ghost-humping me, too.

Walking up the shop aisle, I think to catch him in the act. Teach him a lesson. Put a stop to such lewd antics once and for all. Passing the crisps section, I suddenly spin around and come face-to-face with the Monster! Thankfully, it's just the pickled onion beast on the packet of some Monster Munch. The shopkeeper, to my relief, is still at the counter tapping away at his phone.

At first, I'm relieved, but then I get a little offended that I've been rendered unfit for a ghost hump. What have those grannies got that

I haven't? I'll have to bend over a shopping trolley with my tightest trousers on for him next time so he finds me irresistible.

On my way to the back of the shop to snag a bag of potatoes, I grab a couple of tins of dog food for Pearl, a can of Diet Coke for Rachel, and a packet of the shop's own brand Jaffa Cakes for Rachel's grandad. Making my way back to the counter, I very nearly bump into a young lad, about 16 years old, sweeping the shop floor.

'Sorry, mate,' I say. 'Didn't see you there.'

'Oh, you're alright,' he says, sweeping some dirt into a dustpan. 'Between you and me,' he whispers, looking over his shoulder to check his shopkeeper boss isn't listening, 'I've not tried those own brand jaffas meself, but everyone who buys 'em says they're proper rank.'

'Really?'

'Yep,' the lad says, pushing his curtained brown hair out of his eyes.

'Thanks for your honesty,' I say with a wink, then go put the rank Jaffa Cakes back on the shelf.

As I do, a hooded youth comes through the door, goes straight to the fridges to grab a can of the Monster energy drink, and beats me to the till. Even from a Covid-safe social distance, I can smell the stale stench of cigarettes emanating from his grubby clothes.

'Ten B & H,' he mumbles while counting out some coins in his hands with dance music wheezing out of his headphones.

'We're not having any B & H, sorry,' replies the shopkeeper.

The hoodie, dressed in black from head to toe, drops his shoulders in a huff like his mum's just told him he can't have another bowl of Coco-Pops.

'Lambert and Butler then,' he grunts, pointing a filthy fingernail at a stack of blue packets over the shopkeeper's shoulders.

The youth recounts his coins, then throws them, one by one, in a disrespectful manner for the shopkeeper to scoop up from the counter. With each coin that crashes against the metal tray underneath the protective Covid screen, I can see the rage of indignation reaching boiling point inside the shopkeeper. His cheeks are burning red, his mouth tightening, his top lip twitching. Please! Please don't hump the youth. This won't end well for you!

'Ang-on,' says the scallywag, leaving the till to get something else with the money he seems surprised to have left over.

As the lad turns his back on us to select a sweetie from the chocolate rack, the shopkeeper waves a fist of fury at him behind his back. Then he loses his mind and does something very stupid. Something dangerous. Something some might say is suicidal if the youth is a violent type. With the young lad's back still turned, he runs from behind the till, grabs his can of Monster and starts shaking it like a cocktail mixer. Just like before when he humped the grandma, he's looking at me for some kind of recognition before he stops. I shake my head in pale-faced panic to show him I thinks it's the worst idea he's ever had. The youth turns around while the shopkeeper still has the drink in his hands. Luckily, he's already stopped shaking it up. He pretends to be reading the writing on the can and revolves it a few times before gently putting it down.

'Monster drinks. Monster Munch. Monster Mash. Why is everything about monsters?' he waffles, then straightens the black tie underneath the grey jumper he's wearing.

I take a cautionary step back away from the counter and the shaken-up can as the lad comes back to the till with a Lion Bar. Just as he did before, he tosses his coins at the shopkeeper. Every piece of silver, gold and copper smashes into the metal tray with a cacophonous crash.

The shopkeeper watches on, wearing a crooked smirk knowing justice will be served for his bad-mannered, coin-tossing nemesis.

'Bloody bastards throwing money at me,' he complains once the lad has sloped out of the shop without so much as a please or thank you. 'Do I look like I'm fucking begging for his pocket money?'

'Youth of today, eh?' is all I can think to say.

'You're having a dog?' he asks, bleeping the dog food under the scanner.

'I do indeed.'

'The dog of my neighbour is making shits on my front garden.'

'That's not nice.'

'One day I will throw the shittings in the bloody bastard's hot tub where they're making loud parties,' he vows.

I place my money into his tray very carefully so as not to offend him. I did consider kissing the coins and tickling his palm with them before doing so, but thought that might be overdoing it.

When I get home, potatoes in hand to make the 'Tattie 'Ash' and save the day, Rachel jumps out from behind the kitchen door to scare me. It's one of her favourite tricks and I really should've been expecting it since she does it so regularly. Because I'm in a rush to get back and start peeling the potatoes, she catches me off guard and frightens the living shit out of me.

Once I've put my skin back on after jumping out of it, I tell her about what went down in the shop.

'He was a right little tosser,' I quip about the coin-tossing oik.

'Your dad jokes are getting more painful,' she complains. 'That shopkeeper does sound like a madman, though.'

'He's like most people I've met up here,' I say. 'Barmy.'

Before handing over Rachel's Diet Coke, I copy the method in the shopkeeper's madness and shake the can up. Revenge for her scaring me is not only sweet, but also very sticky.

Chapter 19

Touched by the Wind

'You've got cracking veins!' An A & E nurse complimented me as she took my blood for a test.

'Thanks,' I said, proudly admiring the cracking vein in my arm she pricked with her needle.

After a suspected bout of food poisoning, that's arguably the most exciting day out I've had since coming home and spending most of that time in lockdown.

Now, however, that's all about to change, because there's finally something else to get my cracking veins bubbling with excitement: it's May Bank Holiday weekend and another layer of lockdown has been lifted. Not only are we allowed to leave the house, we're also allowed to leave town again. Travel cross-country, not just cross-town.

Rachel and I dream of stroking seal noses in the Cornwall sea, taming the Beast of Bodmin high up in the Devon moors, or combing the tails of wild ponies in the New Forest. We make a vow to discover new land in our homeland. To boldly go where we've never been before.

So, where do we end up going, I hear you ask?

Shropshire.

With international travel all but impossible and staycations in high demand, it's our only available and affordable option.

I know absolutely nothing about Shropshire. What I do know, though, is that it must be the hardest place name to say if you've had a few too many.

'Shrroo. Shhhhhop. Shroo-sheeeeshshshsttt!' Spit, dribble, everyone runs away putting their umbrellas up.

Matters not – off we pop to the shire of the shrop!

In a hired camper van Mavis gave us (my nickname for the rent-a-car company, Avis), we set off late afternoon for the 90-minute drive south. Cruising the country roads towards the Welsh borders, we take in mile upon mile of lurid yellow rapeseed fields; castle ruins crowning fertile, plump hills; canals tinselled in the sunshine spanned by rumbling, shaky bridges that have us bouncing about in our seats like popcorn in a microwave when we drive over them.

We cut through quaint villages with eccentric features like obsolete red phone boxes enchantingly converted into "Book Boxes," crammed from ceiling to floor with second-hand books; giant hedges carefully cut around mini-red Royal Mail postboxes; thatched cottages-cum-antique boutiques.

Sadly, the bright but crisp weather couldn't promise to warm our hearts like the scenery. As we were leaving town, a presenter on BBC Lancashire announced: 'On today, the first of May, it's going to be minus one at midnight. I'll have to put fleeces on me plums!'

Upon hearing that news, Rachel looked up the forecast for Wem, the Shropshire town where we'd be staying. 'Yep, minus one there tonight, too.'

Then, in a moment of nostalgia, she couldn't help but look up the temperature in Tenerife.

'Twenty-six degrees Celsius there today. And minus one here freezing to death,' she reported, sadness about how our lives have changed so dramatically passing over her fallen face.

'Never let your memories be greater than your dreams, baby,' I said.

'What do you mean by that?' she said, sliding her phone into a space under the radio.

'We have to believe the best times will always be ahead of us,' I insist, pulling up the handbrake at a red light.

'Hmmm,' Rachel replies with more than a hint of scepticism.

'Joe Biden didn't fulfil his dream of becoming American President until he was 78.'

'Really?'

'Yep. And, if you want some inspiration from a Boltonian, Joe Foster, the owner of Reebok, didn't have his business take off until well into his 50s.'

'I didn't know that,' she says, starting to come round as the lights turn green.

This uncharacteristic display of self-pity from Rachel is exactly why we needed to get away. The lockdown monotony on top of enduring our first long British winter in many a moon has had us not only spending too much time inside our house, but also our heads feeling sorry for ourselves.

So now, having broken free from our domestic detention, not even the prospect of having to put fleeces on my plums on a cold weekend in a caravan is going to dampen my intrepid, bank holiday spirit. I resolve to remain positive and give us both the lift we so badly need.

Turning into the caravan site at dusk, first impressions are good. There's freshly mown lawns; a crazy golf course; a kids' play area; a hay-filled pen housing bleating goats; an onsite mini supermarket; a reception area; a forecourt of camper vans and caravans with their prices displayed inside the windscreens. And, in a nod to its rural setting, huge parking spaces allocated for "TRACTORS ONLY."

Once checked in, we use a card a receptionist gave me to pass through a barrier and access the caravan park. Now, I know that last sentence was about as interesting as watching grass grow, but please bear with me. You'll soon discover why this seemingly meaningless detail is pivotal.

After passing through the barrier, we chug down a five-mile-per-hour limit gravel track, past a long row of static caravans. On the bottom half they're all pastel green, and on the top half, white. Within the grounds of most are telltale signs that these are second homes, not just holiday homes: family photos on the walls; wooden plaques adorning front doors with surnames carved into them; gnomes, buddhas and dog statues personalising immaculately kept gardens; swing balls swaying in a stiff wind that's having fun spinning the wheels on kid's bikes dropped to the ground; gazebos with tables and chairs set underneath.

We lower the windows to let in some fresh country air, but the nauseating stench of fertiliser from the open farm fields to our left soon has us whirring them right back up again.

With the temperature plummeting towards zero as foretold by the radio presenter, we unload the van as quickly as possible before getting cosy inside. We fire up the heaters, slip into our onesies and settle down for a cosy first night of three in the caravan. My plums are suitably fleeced. I suspect Rachel's apricot is toasty, too.

Setting the scene, Rachel draws the curtains in her cow onesie, lights a scented cinnamon candle and tunes in to Smooth FM. "You're the Best Thing" by the Style Council is playing. In my penguin onesie,

I shuffle the pack for a game of cards and pour two glasses of wine with my right flipper. Pearl chews loudly and open-mouthed on a treat as rain begins to drum on the caravan roof that the cosiness metre is about to go through. Ahhhhh, this is the . . .

BANG BANG BANG!

My peas shrink and freeze with fear. Rachel audibly gasps. Pearl drops her treat onto the floor, sits up and barks! Someone, rather violently, has knocked on the caravan window. I tentatively twitch open the front curtains. Staring me in the face are two maniacal blue eyes.

'That your van?' a man wearing a bright yellow, high-vis jacket and faded blue cap shouts.

'Yeah?' I confirm.

His face temporarily disappears behind his warm breath fogging up the cold window, then reappears like a supernatural spectre.

'You can't bring that thing in 'ere unless you're unloading,' he informs me in no uncertain terms in a lilting Black Country accent.

His face is gone again.

'Really? Why?' I shout back at the fogged up glass.

'It's policy.' He's back again.

Having this conversation through the misty window is getting silly. I slide on my belly along the caravan's laminate flooring in my penguin onesie and go outside.

'The girl in reception just gave me this to get in,' I plead, presenting the all-important card that should render me innocent of any wrong-doing (see, told you, card, pivotal).

'They didn't know you 'ad a van,' he says.

'They didn't ask.'

'You should've said.'

'How was I to know I can't park my own camper van outside my caravan on a campsite?' I ask, flippers wide open in confusion.

'Well, now you know.'

'But there's a van over there,' I observe, nodding at another camper van with my penguin beak.

'That's one's got windows in the back. Yours has panels.'

'Oh.' I have to take a moment to process this new information. 'I'm not complaining,' I say, doing my best not to sound argumentative, 'I'm just curious. Why are my van's lack of back windows a dealbreaker?'

'It's policy,' he repeats.

'It's bollocks,' I want to reply, but wisely swallow the thought.

'Follow me back to the entrance and I'll show you where to leave your van,' he orders.

Continuing to bite my lip, I do as I'm told. Walking in front of my hire van like a funeral director would a hearse, he marches me back to a parking area near the entrance. Following him on foot whilst driving at an unnaturally slow speed of around 3-4mph in first gear, I stall the van twice. It's extremely humiliating and brings back memories of my first driving lesson with my diabetic instructor, Alan Pitcher. I couldn't tell if it was my bad driving or his sugar levels that were causing him to sweat, swear and reach for his sucky sweets.

The next morning when I take Pearl for a walk around the grounds of the caravan site, an A4 "PARK RULES" laminate pinned to a notice board grabs my attention. Amongst 26 bullet-pointed, capitalised and underlined "MUST NOTS" in bold, there's a few intriguing ones. None more so than these two:

NO POSTING PHOTOS OF THE SWIMMING
POOL ON FACEBOOK

NO CHINESE FIRE LANTERNS ALLOWED
ON THE PARK AT ANY TIME

Could these "MUST NOTS" get any more random? I think of a few more unlikely eventualities I could add to the list for fun:

NO SLEEPING ON THE DANCE FLOOR

NO COOKING LIVER AND ONIONS ON
TUESDAYS

NO CATS ON SKIS

I read on the caravan park's webpage before leaving that the site was an American army camp during World War II. Seems that influence still remains. The place feels more like a boot camp than a holiday camp.

Searching for somewhere more relaxed with fewer rules, we use our phones to locate a country park a short drive away. Not long after, we're jumping out of the van on a dead-end country lane leading into some dense woods. At the entrance, we're faced with yet more behavioural warnings. On another A4 laminate taped to a kissing gate, it says:

THOUGHTLESS DOG OWNERS WE'RE
WATCHING YOU! 9/10 OWNERS CLEAN UP
AFTER THEIR PETS. WILL YOU BE THE ONE
WHO DOESN'T?

Above the message is a very scary pair of eyes. They look like they belong to a species part wolf, part man and part eagle. Not to dissimilar from the crazy eyes I saw glaring at me through the caravan window at me last night.

We walk into the woods on eggshells.

'So different down here, ain't it?' I whisper to Rachel, keeping my voice down just in case someone watching us can hear us.

'What do you mean?'

'Our local country park up north gives you the lowdown on the history, wildlife and flora when you enter,' I say. 'Just over an hour south, and all we get are warnings.'

'I know, I don't like it,' Rachel says, scanning the spaces between the myriad tree trunks for anyone that might be spying on us. I keep an eye on the sky just in case there's a drone following us.

The odd characters we encounter in the country park don't help to put us at ease. We bump into a young couple and ask them if we're going the right way for a lookout point we read about that has views to the Welsh mountains. Both of them say nothing in reply but stand mute and motionless with blank, empty stares. They look right through us like we're not even there.

Deeper into the park, walking between head-high corn fields on both sides, we say hello to a senior couple dressed in countryside tweed as we overtake them. Same as the people from earlier, they stare into space and refuse to acknowledge our existence.

When we get further ahead, I steal a glance at them back over my shoulder and see the man has a huge bird of prey perched on his right hand.

'He's got a bird,' I say to Rachel under my breath.

'Don't talk about women like that,' Rachel replies.

'I mean, a real bird, with feathers and wings and claws. One that can shit on your shoulder from the sky.'

'Don't swear!' Rachel tells me off before sneaking a peek. 'It looks like it could peck people to death with that beak,' she says, quickening her pace.

'Beak? It's more like a bayonet!' I say.

The bird of prey catches me stealing another look and makes an "I'm gonna slit your throat" gesture, running a sharp claw across its neck.

'Let's get out of here!' I say, beginning to walk as fast as I can without actually starting to run.

In our haste to get away from the evil avian and find our way back to the van, we get lost. The area is a maze of trees and steep, sandy paths shooting off in various directions through overgrown bushes, nettles and weeds. Our phones have lost reception, too. We're up Weirdo Hill without a paddle.

As we sit on some fallen tree trunks and take a moment to retrace our steps, we see the young zombie couple from earlier coming up the hill towards us. I make another attempt to contact the living.

'Excuse me,' I say, stepping in front of them so they have to at least make eye contact. 'Does that path you're on take us to where we saw you earlier? We're trying to get back to our van.'

The girl stares past me into the middle distance. The lad makes eye contact with me this time but still says nothing.

'Is that the same path we just saw you on?' I try again.

'Yeah, we did see you earlier,' the lad mutters back without actually answering my question.

'Okay. Thanks,' I say.

'They're dressed like they're going clubbing later,' Rachel says. 'I reckon they're on something.'

'Whatever it is, it ain't the planet.'

Through much trial and error, we eventually find our way back to the van. We're more on edge than before after having those brief yet unsettling encounters with the villagers and getting lost up in the hills.

'There's a town called Whitchurch 10 minutes away,' I say to Rachel, starting up the engine and locking the doors. 'Maybe the people there will be more normal.'

Whitchurch is a pretty little town. Church bells chime every quarter hour; the smell of hot pies and pasties is piped out from bakeries onto the high street dotted with art studios; gourmet food and drink shops and family-run cafés with dog biscuits in jars set on outside tables add a touch of charm. The locals we mix with though, just like the folk we met earlier in the woods, are, for want of a better word, peculiar.

On our way into the town centre on a very narrow pavement, a man up ahead suddenly turns around and starts walking directly at us, very nearly forcing us onto the road and into the path of oncoming traffic. Again, like we don't exist. Like we're not even there. To another stranger, who walks unnaturally close to me as he passes, I say, 'You alright, mate?'

He stops, scratches his head and says, 'Think so!' in a West Country accent.

I'm not convinced.

'You remember I told you I lived in Menorca for a year before I moved to Tenerife?' I ask Rachel.

'Yep,' she says, pushing the WAIT button at a traffic light.

'They've got a local saying for weird people like this. They say they're "touched by the wind."'

Something in the water or the wind, there most definitely is. And, it would appear that the security guards in the caravan park have been touched by it too, because two of them are baying for our blood upon our return. The one who looks like Freddie Mercury's older, balder brother is the first to speak.

'Van! Move it! Now,' he thunders outside our caravan.

'But the other guy said last night I could bring it in to unload,' I protest while grabbing our shopping from the back of the van.

'No he didn't!'

'He bloody did!'

'You were told last night not to bring the van in 'ere,' he says, aggressively putting his face right up to mine. His breath smells like the bin men have been on strike for a month.

'Unless I'm unloading,' I say, standing my ground. 'Which I'm doing now with my shopping,' I add, holding up Morrisons bags with both hands to prove it. 'I was going to drive it straight back out again.'

'You drove it in 'ere at 11 o'clock this morning and it's been 'ere ever since,' he lies through the gaps in his black teeth.

'That's not true. You've just seen me drive back in from being out all day.'

'Move it or I'll have it towed,' he threatens with a bit of spit bubbling on his moustache.

As I take a deep breath to centre myself so I don't say or do something I'll regret (like pull on his protruding nose hairs), I notice we've attracted an unwanted audience. The second-homers have come out of the surrounding caravans and they're all standing on their outside decking, arms folded, looking at us like we've only got ourselves to blame. One man is eating Hula Hoops off his six fingers.

We retreat back inside our caravan somewhat shaken where we take a seat and try to calm down.

'This is ridiculous,' Rachel says, giving Pearl a comfort hug.

'I know,' I agree. 'Are some friendly faces and to feel at home away from home too much to ask?'

Then the truth hits me in the face like that security guard's bin breath just did.

'You know what?' I say, standing up. 'We already have that up north.'

Soon after, we drive the van back out of the caravan park as we were told to do. And never come back.

Sometimes you've got to go away to appreciate what you already have at home.

Chapter 20

Risky Business

Every now and again, life can throw up some painfully awkward scenarios: accidentally touching the hand of the person next to you on public transport (CRINGE!); getting harassed by a wasp and having to repel it without looking scared even though you're about to burst out crying; asking someone for assistance in a shop only to find out they don't actually work there.

You get the picture. It's a social minefield out there where embarrassment could blow up in your face around the next corner.

A corner that I'm about to turn.

Since falling ill with suspected salmonella poisoning, I've been raining out of my rectum for a good few weeks now. I'm getting a lot worse when I should be getting better.

I'd love to be like Bunion Beryl and liberally share graphic details about my ailment to the first person who may care to listen, but that's not how I've been brought up. As a youngster down south, I'd been reared to only discuss the derrière with close confidants behind closed doors.

'It's not the sorta fing you go around shoutin' your mouth off about, Bradley,' my mum would chide me when I thought it was funny to bring up arse matters over the dinner table as a little bin lid.[1] Suffice to say, mum has since been the word when issues of this kind have arisen.

After a phone consultation with an Advanced Nursing Practitioner, she advised me to 'go fetching' a test tube and a spatula from my local GP surgery so they can test my stool.

Ordinarily, I'd have thought disclosing my problem confidentially where this is a patient's legal right would be easy, but when I arrive, the surgery is full of people and a hive of activity. Finding the right person to tell this sensitive and personal information to is not going to be as straightforward as I hoped. Locals in high-vis jackets are marshalling people forming an orderly queue in the car park that's stretching around the corner and onto the streets. Nurses in masks, pink uniforms and plastic white aprons are darting in and out of the entrance. The car park barrier is locked down and long lines of cars are reverse parking on both sides of the street outside. There's that many people and vehicles around that it looks like a pop concert is about to start.

I walk past the queues towards the car park barrier where a friendly looking elder gent is standing with a walkie-talkie in his hand.

'You 'aff stand ont' green spots or alligators get you,' he informs me, pointing to the green social distancing markers on the ground.

'Is this the queue to get in the surgery?' I ask him, hoping the answer is no.

'It's the queue for the vaccines,' he says.

'They're playing a gig, are they?' I joke.

'You what?'

---

1. Cockney rhyming slang for "kid".

'The band. The Vaccines,' I pun. 'Is that what all the fuss is about?'

'I've not a bloomin' clue what you're going on about.'

'Sorry, bad joke,' I apologise. 'The Vaccines are a famous rock band.'

'They can't be that famous, I've never heard of 'em.'

'I'll stop talking nonsense and get straight to the point,' I say. 'I'm not here for the vaccine. I've been sent by a nurse to pick something up.'

'Oh, right,' he says, sounding surprised. 'Ang-on, I'll tell 'em.'

'Thanks.'

'I've got a man outside 'ere,' the man with glasses and short, grey curly hair reports into his walkie-talkie. 'Says he's been sent by a nurse to pick up summat.'

'Which nurse?' crackles back a female voice.

'Which nurse?' he asks.

'Erm. Carol Burton.'

'Carol Burton,' he says.

'Okay, let 'im in then.'

'How come they're doing the vaccinations at the surgery?' I quiz the man.

'They bring em 'ere once a month for old buggers like me that can't go very far.'

'Great idea,' I say as he waves me through.

'And, be careful o' alligators,' he quips, pointing to green markers on the ground.

Through the white, double entry doors with porthole-style windows, I spy a waiting room full of what looks like masked workers and volunteers. They're all sat on chairs getting a briefing from a lady at the front holding a clipboard.

With trepidation, I quietly push the doors open, trying not to interrupt them in their quest to help vaccinate the community. Normally I'd head straight for the reception window, but the shutters are down. Instead, I shyly stand at the back, wondering where and how I can locate the nurse, Carol Burton, then squirt some sanitiser onto my hands. With the scent of its cleansing chemicals sneaking up my nostrils, I wait patiently while the authoritative lady in charge at the front directs proceedings.

'We're opening in 20 minutes,' she updates the room at the top of her voice. 'Em-leh!' she cries. 'Can you check all't booths are read-eh?'

Emily gets booth checking.

'Tray-ceh!' she yells with a hand in the air to get Tracey's attention. 'Can you be going taking temperatures at door-waz?'

Tracey grabs her thermometer checking gun and heads to the doors where I'm stood looking lost.

'You volunteering?' Tracey asks.

'No I'm –'

'You shouldn't be 'ere then,' she sternly informs me.

'But . . . I've been told to come in by Carol Burton.'

'For what reason?'

'Um . . . Carol will know if you tell her my name. We had a phone consultation about half an hour ago.'

'Can you not tell me worri'tis? We're bizz-eh!'

'I'd rather not say in front of all these people,' I say sheepishly. 'Carol knows.'

'Riiiight,' she exhales with a despairing shake of the head. 'I need teck your temperature if you want to come in,' she insists, pointing her temperature checking gun at my forehead.

'Go for it,' I say, leaning towards her.

'Riiight . . . You're alriiight,' she says, checking the reading. 'Wait over there out'ta way, and I'll go find Carol,' she says, pointing to the corner of the waiting room. 'And keep your face covering on, please.'

'Will do,' I promise.

This unexpected delay is making me even more nervous because time is very much of the essence. I've been crying muddy rivers out of my arse at the most random and inconvenient of times. I need to get in and out of here as quick as I can before nature knocks at my backdoor again.

As instructed, I make my way to the corner where there's a life-sized cardboard cutout of a balding male pensioner wearing glasses and a green cardigan. He's holding a piece of card that says:

"I KNOW MY RISK, DO YOU KNOW YOURS?"

I most certainly do. Mine is that my stomach could fall out at any moment.

The lady in charge continues commanding the mission. She's ticking things off her clipboard, firing orders to various personnel and answering questions and queries coming in from all angles. She shakes her head at some, frowns at others and bulges her eyes after someone whispers in her ears. Could this be Carol? I daren't trouble her if it is.

After five minutes or so stood next to Len, as I've named the cardboard cutout pensioner who knows his risk, I've still not been attended to. The whole time I've been praying that the relentless waves of stomach cramps don't turn into a poo-nami flooding out of my trapdoor. Try as I might to stop it happening, I can't help but pass wind to relieve the pressure building in my stomach. As Rachel says when she does a panty whisper, 'It's just air,' and thankfully is not accompanied by an unpleasant whiff.

Waiting in the corner with cardboard cutout Len washes up unhappy memories of being put on lunchtime detention and made to stand in the corner of the school office. Every time this happened, I had to watch our headmaster subconsciously pick his nose and eat it in his office. That's why me and my mates renamed Mr Dixon, Mr Picks 'Em.

Len pokes me in the arm and strikes up a conversation.

'What you in for?' he asks.

'Food poisoning. Proper bad bout. I've even had to give up football training cos I've lost two stone and haven't got the energy,' I answer. 'What you in for, Len?'

'Just 'ere raising profile o' Type 2 Diabetes,' he says proudly. 'They pay me in pies.'

'Sounds like a cushty gig,' I say.

'You ont' loo a lot?' he asks.

'Len, my friend,' I say, putting my arm around him, 'I've had so much ring action recently, I'm thinking of changing my name to Frodo.'

'Ha! I love *Lord of the Rings*, me!' Len says.

'Problem is, Len, I'm not the lord of mine,' I lament.

'Bloomin 'eck, is that you?' Len says, abruptly moving away from me.

'Sorry,' I say, covertly wafting away the smell of steamed broccoli, 'that'll be me dicky tummy.'

That one wasn't just air. It was nigh on chemical warfare.

After a quarter of an hour exiled in the naughty corner chatting to Len, it becomes apparent that with everything that's going on, Tracey's forgotten to tell Carol that I'm waiting. I'm going to have to be brave enough to leave my corner spot, pray that my farts don't turn into sharts[2] and approach a member of staff to remind them that I'm waiting for Carol. I'll have to do it without appearing pushy, impatient or looking like I'm afraid my bottom could break at any moment.

I cautiously move away from my naughty spot and head for the reception desk which has now opened. The second I dare to make a move, I'm put back in my place by a nurse.

'Erm,' she says with a hand in my face, ordering me to stop in my tracks. 'Can I help you, sir?'

'I've been asked to come in by Carol. Carol Burton.'

'What, today, on vaccination day, sir?'

'Yeah! We just spoke on the phone. She told me to quickly pop in and pick something up,' I repeat.

'Worr'is it? A prescription?'

'No. She'll know what it's about if you tell her my name,' I say.

'IS CAROL THERE?' she bellows across the noisy waiting room to the receptionist who wheels her chair back, stands up and cranes her neck.

'SHE'S BIZZ-EH!'

'THIS MAN'S LOOKING FOR 'ER,' the nurse shouts back, pointing at me. 'SAYS SHE'S TOLD 'IM COME IN.'

'WHAT'S 'IS NAME?' booms the receptionist.

'What's your name?'

'My name's Bradley Ch –'

'HIS NEM'S BRAD-LEH!'

'BRAD-LEH WHAT?' the receptionist asks.

'Brad-leh what?' the nurse asks, turning back to me.

---

2. When the passing of wind triggers the passing of a stool, hence the portmanteau, "shart" (shit/fart).

'Chermside,' I say, quietly trying to get her to mirror my hushed tones so I can get back under the radar.

'CHERMSIDE,' the nurse shouts to the receptionist.

'YOU WHAT?' the receptionist quizzes, unable to process my surname. 'GERM-I-SIDE?'

'NO. CH. CHERMSIDE,' the nurse corrects her.

'ANG-ON,' the receptionist shouts back, clacking my name into her keyboard.

I bow my head to hide the fact that my eyes are rolling due to the painful inefficiency of it all. If I hadn't sensed a seismic bowel movement was about to send the sphincter scale soaring, I would have jumped over the desk, found Carol myself, then shook her by the shoulders and pleaded:

'Please hurry up and give me the fucking test tube and spatula because my arse is about to go off like a fire extinguisher.'

'HAS HE GOT A DATE OF BIRTH?' the receptionist yells.

'Have you got a date of birth?' the nurse asks.

'Of course I've got a date of birth,' I'm about to bark. But then the receptionist shouts, 'S'OKAY! I'VE FEAUWND HIM.'

The noisy room full of staff and volunteers has quietened down and zoomed in on our three-way conversation. Myself, the nurse and the receptionist now have a large audience. Every single person in the room is hanging on the receptionist's next word.

'STOO-WOOL SAMPLE!' the receptionist broadcasts.

'STOO-WOOL SAMPLE?' repeats the nurse by my side.

'YEAH. CAROL WANTS A STOO-WOOL SAMPLE.'

A masked old lady makes a squirm face I'll never forget. It's an expression that says, 'Ooh, I bet he wishes the ground would swallow him up.'

The crap is out of the bag.

Chapter 21

Hat Trick

'That's the one,' I eavesdrop one lady say to another as I walk past them chatting on a doorstep during my lunch break.

At first, I think nothing of it and automatically assume the pensioners are talking about someone else. But then, as Pearl stops to sniff some grass across the road from the house they're stood outside, I notice one of them pointing at me. Just like I did when I was being talked about by the swimming pool staff, I wonder what I could've done to attract their attention.

As a gent walks by whistling and swinging an umbrella like Gene Kelly, I touch my forehead to see if I've absent-mindedly put my snorkel on my head to do the dog walk. I haven't. I check to see if I have any wet patches in places that might court controversy. I don't. Are my flies open? No, the cage where my Manaconda lives is firmly zipped up.

I decide to call their bluff. Show them that it's not okay to gossip about a new member of their community and make them feel paranoid like this. I have my rights as a law-abiding, tax-paying citizen. I'm not quite sure what they are when it comes to two senior citizens talking about me, but I'm going to take a stand nonetheless. There

must be some Citizens Charter on a scroll somewhere in the town hall
that's got my back. As former First Lady Eleanor Roosevelt once said,
"Great minds discuss ideas, small minds gossip."

It's time to call them out.

I cross the quiet residential back street and walk directly towards the
bungalow where the grey-haired ladies are stood outside talking about
me in their dressing gowns.

When they see me coming for them, they look pleased. As if they've
been expecting me. With the sound of their fluffy slippers scuffing
down the concrete garden path, they walk towards me.

It's two against one. I scan about their persons for anything they
could use to do damage. They're both armed with dressing gown cords
with which they could strangle me; the woman who pointed at me has
a knitting needle in her dressing gown pocket she could use to gouge
my eyes out; and her mate has a teaspoon in her hand that she could
smack me on the head with like a hard-boiled egg.

Pearl declares herself not arsed and continues sniffing the grass. I
lock her extendable lead and give it a gentle tug to encourage her to
get moving. I'm going to need her on my side should they try use their
dressing gown cords, knitting needles or teaspoons to draw blood.

Just as I'm preparing for battle on the frontline where garden path
meets pavement, one of them, the pointy woman, shows they come in
peace.

'Ee's little cutie, ent' eh?' she coos at Pearl trotting across the road
to catch me up from behind.

'She certainly is,' I agree, approaching with caution to make sure
this isn't small talk to lull me into a false sense of security before they
attack.

'Oooh, it's a she. How old is she?' Mrs Pointer asks.

'We're not sure. She's a rescue from Spain, so we don't know her age. The vets thinks she's about seven or eight.'

'Oooh, you've done a good thing,' the other lady says.

'Was an easy decision,' I reply. 'She's the spits of the dog I had as a kid. How could I not rescue her?'

'Oooh, you're not from reauwnd 'ere, are ya?' Mrs Pointer insinuates, pressing her glasses to her nose to get a clearer look at me.

''Fraid not!'

'You sound all posh,' her friend observes.

'Posh? You must be joking! I'm from Essex.'

'You're not off that programme, are you? *The Only Way Is Essex*,' Mrs Pointer implies.

'No chance. I watched it once for five minutes. That was more than enough.'

'Are you all like that down there?' she asks.

'Like what?'

'You know . . . big lips and balloons int' blouses.'

'Well, I've not got any,' I joke, pressing my hands to my flat chest.

'That lot o-wer there are like it,' Mrs Pointer says, pointing three doors up to a spectacular, high-spec, three-storey house with a mirror glass façade towering over the surrounding bungalows. Outside on an expansive driveway, there's a black Range Rover with a female name making up the first four characters on its personalised registration plate. The last three letters are "Y-M-M." Something tells me they stand for "Yummy Mummy."

'They're out here ont' street alt'time. Bloody lips and tits, they are,' Mrs Pointer complains.

'Oh well, if it makes them feel better about themselves,' I counter.

'They've got cockney accents as well like you,' she says, bending over to pull out a weed in the garden path.

'Have they really?' I say, surprised to find out I'm not the only southern cat amongst the northern pigeons.

'Eh!' Mrs Pointer cuts in, brusquely changing the subject. 'I were just talking to Jean 'ere about you.'

Jean, who has every single nail painted a different colour, nods and raises her eyebrows to back her up.

'Were you?'

'Yeah . . . I were saying you're the one that wears your hat t'other way round.'

'Do I!' I check, then self-consciously put my cap back on the right way round.

'Yeah . . . I see you walking past 'ere from time to time with your lovely little dog, hat on t'other way round, wondering why you wear it like that?'

'Good question?' I ponder, having never been asked this before.

'I said to Jean, "I wonder why he wears his hat t'other way round like that."'

'I said it must make you go faster,' Jean jokes.

'Haha! Maybe it does?' I consider. 'Next time I'm in a rush, I'll give it a try,' I say, incredulous that even the grannies up north are full of banter, jibes and capable of giving complete strangers like me a good ribbing.

Whilst I also struggle to fathom that wearing my cap backwards has got the locals' chins wagging, Pearl has other things on her mind. She wanders over to a lamp post a few feet away, arches her back into a cat stretch and prepares to do a very terrible thing. Oh god. Why here? Why now, in full view of the garrulous grannies?

'Nooooo,' I try in a bargaining tone, pulling her away. 'Not here, Pearl.'

'Pearl, what a lovely name,' Jean says.

I start to walk away from the ladies and hope Pearl will follow. She doesn't. It's too late. She's got the digestive biscuit rolling and has committed to finishing the job, here and now, in front of Mrs Pointer and Jean.

'If you've gotta go, you've gotta go,' Jean pardons, offering Pearl the green light to deliver the brown.

'Don't mind us,' says Mrs Pointer, waving a magnanimous hand. 'We all need do do-dos.'

I thank them for understanding with a nervous, apologetic laugh while Pearl tries as hard as she can but fails to produce a single pellet. Nothing's happening. It's just me, Mrs P and Rainbow Nails Jean watching Pearl strain at the foot of a lamppost but draw blanks. God, this is awkward.

I consider putting my cap on Pearl's head backwards to make her go faster but before I can, she scurries away from us and strains some more – to no avail. She does it again. Four, agonising times: scurries a few feet, strains for a good few seconds, then, when nothing happens, makes intense eye contact with all three of us in a cry for help. As Mrs Pointer and Jean watch with great interest to see how this will play out, Pearl sprints at them and it's only then do I see what all the fuss is about.

Pearl's odd behaviour is down to a nugget that's matted in the hairs around her hoop. She's now wagging her stubby tail at the ladies, hoping they might be able to help her remove it. From where they're standing, they can't see what I can see. They think she wants a stroke when she actually wants them to stick their hands between the back of her legs and evict the "hanger-on."

I have to do something before the ladies get their hands on Pearl and dog shit all over their dressing gowns. In a panic, I slip my hand into the specially assigned bag I have on my person for this task and plunge my hand between Pearl's back legs. It's the only way to dislodge the swinging excrement matted in her hair. Problem is, it's not giving. It's cemented in there. The ladies' faces quickly turn from confused to concerned as they compute the abject horror that, from their angle, must look like I've got my hand up Pearl's bottom as I attempt to yank the offending object free.

'You okay there?' Jean asks, backing away from me up the garden path.

'It got stuck,' I say, tying a knot in the plastic bag. I don't know why, but I bounce the loaded poop bag up and down in the air like I've just won a goldfish at a fun fair.

'Things ya do, eh?' I say, then put my cap on backwards again to get out of there as fast as I can before they call the RSPCA.

Chapter 22

Two Upmanship

In his book about living in England, *Notes From a Small Island*, American Bill Bryson writes, "If you want to know your shortcomings, you won't find more helpful people than those from Yorkshire."

I'm able to test out this theory when I get to work with a Yorkshireman, thanks to my long-awaited return to the entertainment industry.

The gentleman in question is a DJ for a wedding reception I'll be singing at. I've been asked to get in touch with him by the bride-to-be. All I need to do is make a quick call to confirm that my singing equipment can plug into his DJ gear. Easy, right? Wrong! The DJ has other ideas.

I try calling him several times but he doesn't answer. It seems people just don't want to talk these days, and most prefer to message or voice note. A 2015 study suggested that this is not a good move if you want to live a happy life. It concluded that limited face-to-face social contact nearly doubles someone's risk of having depression. The same study also found that meeting regularly with family and friends reduces symptoms of depression. So the very pertinent takeaway after years of lockdown is, let's get out of the house and get those chins wagging in each other's faces, people!

Hoping for the next best thing to face-to-face contact, I try calling the DJ again a few more times but still can't get through to him. In the end, I give up trying to call and message him instead:

> I'm Brad, the singer for Kim and Lee's wedding. Just trying to arrange sound/tech check times etc... call me back when you can:)

Seconds later, a message comes back:

> What cable do you use for your backing tracks?

I send him a picture of my cable. He quickly replies:

> Mine's better

I'm soon sent a picture of his cable in return. It appears to be pretty much the same as mine, but, somehow, better.

Oh god, what kind of person boasts about a cable? I have a horrible feeling that I've crossed paths with a type of social animal I fear. A social animal that's an expert at one-upmanship; astute at highlighting your shortcomings just like the Yorkshire folk Bill Bryson wrote about in *Notes From a Small Island*. They're the kind of people who, if you've been to Tenerife, they've been to Eleven-erife. They are the dreaded "Topper." I play up to his suspected superiority complex when I reply:

> That's a corker of a cable. Just what I need to plug in and get singing. Am I okay to use it, please?

> Aye I'll let yer. I've also got 14 guitars.

During the next few minutes my phone pings repeatedly like a fruit machine paying out a jackpot. Each one is a photo of a different guitar. This has absolutely no relevance to us working together, but I roll with it nonetheless and jest:

> *That's just showing off.*

He hits me back with a cold, hard, worrying radio silence.

Looks like he didn't get it. Looks like he thinks I think that he really is showing off. Looks like I've upset him.

See, this is the problem with messaging. The real sentiment of my words would have resonated in the light-hearted tone of my voice if we were talking on the phone; would have been understood by a playful slap on the shoulder if we were face-to-face. But messaging through our smartphones, there's been a disconnect.

I hurriedly send a message back to try and smooth things over.

> *You'll make me look like an amateur with your 14 guitars cos I'll just have the one mi-crophone with me.*

He replies, quick sharp.

> *I've got two mics. They're rather nice tbh*

Topped by the "Topper" again! My lord, this is hard work already. I really don't need to see pictures of all his equipment, know all the musical instruments he plays or how many microphones and guitars he has. All I need to know is that our devices are compatible. Since we've already established this thanks to the picture he sent of his incredible cable, it's job done and time to close the lines of communication.

> *Sorry, gotta get back to work. We'll catch up nearer the time to finalise soundcheck times. Nice guitars by the way :)*

I get another notification before I can put my phone down.

> *They call me DJ Bungalow because I've not got a lot up top!*

I'm assuming he's inferring that he's not the brightest light at the disco, but I dare not ask any further questions. I could be here all day looking at his random pictures and counting his musical instruments. I mute the conversation and check back later.

When my work is done for the day, I tentatively reopen my messages. I have 38 waiting to be read from DJ Bungalow. Thirty, fucking, eight! The first says:

> *I've been making lights for my DJ rig*

Attached to the message is a photo of some disco lights. They're sitting on a kitchen worktop next to a bowl containing some onions, potatoes, a tape measure and a variety of other tools – spanners, pliers, Allen keys. I mean, who keeps their onions and potatoes in a bowl with their tools? Who is this madman? And, do I have time to sift through the 30-odd remaining messages from DJ Bungalow? I don't, but curiosity gets one over on me.

He's forwarded photos of "clients I've worked with": a bride being carried in the arms of four groomsmen; two smiling women in ballgowns; an up-nostril selfie of him with another frightened looking man he's got in a playful headlock.

> *This is Nathan from Brother Beyond.*

Even though I've never heard of the band Brother Beyond (research later tells me they had a top-ten hit in the UK with *Get Even* in the late 80s), I give his topper ego another stroking.

> *Rubbing shoulders there mate!*

He immediately pings back:

> *I've sung with better.*

Why am I not surprised? He's got superior cables, has sung with better singers than those who've topped the charts, possesses more microphones. Dearie me. He's not done yet, either. Messages 39 and 40 are incoming.

> *Yep. I work with lots of live acts. Don't worry I've got all the gear.*

Next, he sends a video of him playing guitar. Which I'm assuming is better than all of those that Eric Clapton plays.

I was looking forward to getting back on stage, but now I'm dreading having to deal with a turbo Topper when I do.

***

On the evening of the gig, the satnav has me following directions to a venue in Headingley, Yorkshire. My jaw drops when I pull up at the security gates outside and realise I'm actually singing at the iconic venue that is Headingley Cricket Stadium. Fred Trueman, Geoffrey Boycott, Michael Vaughan – just three of many great Yorkshiremen who've played here and made cricketing history. And tonight, I'll be playing here with another great Yorkshireman, DJ Bungalow. Okay, we may only be playing in the Corporate Suite, but we're still technically "playing" here. Pass me another straw to clutch, will you?

Bug-eyed at the historic surroundings and the hallowed cricketing turf, I close the car door in the parking area, then spot DJ Bungalow unloading his van. Doing what any musician who has a good team ethic does, I offer to help him unload.

'You must be DJ Bungalow,' I say to the very tall, plump and completely bald man doubled over and shifting gear around in the back of his Transit van.

"Correct!" he affirms, out of breath and wiping sweat from his brow. 'I've not got a lot up top,' he reminds me, knocking a fist on the side of his head.

'I'm sure that's not true,' I say. 'I'm Brad. Need a hand?'

'If you don't mind,' he accepts.

He seems really nice and approachable so far. Maybe he just likes to chat, and it's me that's being cold by not wanting to engage in conversation outside of the job at hand. Maybe he's just being stereotypically northern and friendly and chatty and I'm fulfilling the southern stereotype – aloof, uptight and always in a rush.

As we engage in small talk while hauling the equipment up the stairs together, I feel a stab of guilt for having been so quick to judge him.

Once the equipment has been unloaded and set up in the Corporate Suite, the trumpet blowing restarts and I find out it's not me, it's most definitely him.

'How'd you know the bride and groom then?' he asks, taking a seat on a stall next to me at the bar.

'They saw me perform in Tenerife, then asked me to sing at their wedding,' I say, taking a sip from my pint of tap water.

'I picked up three gigs round' pool int' t'Egypt, once,' he brags, throwing pork scratchings into the back of his mouth.

Here we go again . . . I got one, he got three.

''Ow long were you in Tenerife then?' he asks, chewing loudly with his mouth open.

'Nearly 10 years.'

'My oldest was conceived in Tenerife,' he says.

'Congratulations,' I say, surprised he didn't say that he'd been there for 11 years.

'I bet you've played in some reet shit 'oles over there,' he says, jumping off his bar stool to playfully tickle me in the ribs like an uncle might with a nephew.

'Go on, admit it,' he says, intensifying the tickling. 'You have, 'aven't you? You must've played in some reet shit'oles.' He shouts it this time.

'Hahahahahaa! Not wrong!' I giggle, fighting off his rib tickles. 'Shall we do the sound check?' I jump off my stall so I don't wet myself from his tickling.

'We shall,' he says, then makes for the mixing desk.

Grabbing his microphone, he insists on singing me a song.

'Hey! Sit down listen to this,' he says. 'I've been practising.'

This is not the norm. I should be singing in the sound check because I'm doing the singing tonight, not him. I inwardly sigh and sit down at a table on the edge of the dance floor to listen to him sing.

He presses play on his laptop and the intro to "Don't Let the Sun Go Down on Me" by George Michael and Elton John kicks in. As the song moves into the first verse, not only does he sing, he starts to serenade me. DJ Bungalow is now looking into my eyes, singing the first verse at me like his next move is going to be getting down on one knee and asking for my hand in marriage. This is sooooooo weird. Why is he singing at me? Why is he serenading me? I've done thousands of gigs and worked with countless DJs. None of them have ever done this. So why is he doing this?

'Sounds great!' I say, thumbs up, hoping a compliment will make him stop looking into my eyes like he wants to mount me.

'Told you. I've got all the gear,' he boasts over the mic.

The scary thing is, I'm actually starting to like him serenading me and I fear we're now one chorus away from falling in love. I mean, how could I not? I'm only human after all. He's actually got a nice voice. He's the best at everything, has better everything and more of everything than everyone else on the planet. Can you blame me for succumbing?

'But losing everything is like the sun going down on me,' he sings dreamily into my eyes, closing the first chorus.

Those words, "going down on me," evoke some disturbing images in my head and force me to come to my senses. I must end this madness once and for all, or we might end up conceiving here in Headingley like he did in Tenerife. We'll have to call our baby "Stump" in a nod to its cricketing conception.

I get up and walk away while he's serenading me. I make for the speakers and stride purposefully between them, pretending to check they're both working. He follows me, still singing at me all the while.

'You can use this mic, if you want,' he offers.

'I won't share mics because of Covid,' I shout back over the music. 'I've had my two jabs, by the way,' I don't know why I feel the need to disclose.

'I've had three!' he shouts triumphantly on the mic.

Well, what do you know? I've come up short yet again! Never a truer word, Bill Bryson!

Chapter 23

Bad Omen

'You shit b'stard!' a little boy shouts and points at a man three times his size and age.

'Tell your mate, he's not got a bloody clue,' an irate man bawls and salivates.

'Sit down! Shut up!' a big, boisterous group of grown adults demands of a similarly big and boisterous group directly opposite.

If you were thinking I'm at the Houses of Parliament on "Bring Your Kids To Work Day," that'd be a bloody good guess, but not quite right. I am in fact at another kind of mad house – a football match.

Football matches can be tense occasions when the atmosphere is often on a knife edge and normal, everyday behaviour is frequently substituted with unfiltered anger, irrational joy and disproportionate sorrow . . . all because 11 players succeed or fail at forcing a football into a steel and aluminium frame, eight feet high by 24 feet wide. Totally nonsensical, but beautifully bonkers, I'm sure you'll agree.

Although football stadiums harbour a sub-society of deranged supporter beasts that can bring the worst out of people (guilty as charged), they're also home to a lot of beautiful moments too. They're unfolding all around me as the seats start to fill up for kick off – a mother pointing around the ground and whispering to her bug-eyed little boy explanations of everything that's happening; aspiring young footballers dressed in full kit reading the Q&As with their favourite players in the matchday programme while draining their Capri Suns; frail and elderly supporters being helped up and down the stadium steps by fellow fans, family members and stewards; and generations of supporters sat together. Rachel's brother, father and grandad are prime examples. They've all sat together in the same seats since Bolton Wanderers' new stadium first opened in 1997.

Their enthusiasm for traipsing off to see the Wanderers typifies how most Bolton fans feel about their local club. In a recent survey, 69% of fans said their relationship with the club was stronger than ever, while over 70% of fans said the matchday experience was either above average, very good or excellent. Since Bolton have descended down the divisions in the last decade to the rock bottom tier of English football, it can be assumed that this positive sentiment has everything to do with the club's excellent community outreach and nothing to do with the team's success, or lack of it, on the pitch.

It's thanks to my brother-in-law and his fiancée that I'm treated to my very first time watching "the one and only Wanderers," as they're affectionately known.

I first thought accepting their season tickets for Bolton versus Gillingham while they went on holiday was a good idea. That is, until my blood runs cold when I see Mrs Pointer, the lady in my neighbourhood who thinks I wear my cap backwards to go faster and suspects I like to put my hand up my dog's dung dispenser. Even more alarmingly, she's in a position of power and status, working here as a matchday steward! In a bright yellow jacket, she's marshalling and monitoring hundreds of fans in our bottom tier section of the stadium overlooking the halfway line. I spin my cap around and wear it the right way round just like I did when I first met her to try and blend into the crowd and escape her attention.

I'm on tenterhooks as the game gets underway, and I do my best to keep a low profile as Mrs Pointer runs a beady eye over her section of the crowd for any wrongdoers or rule breakers such as people that may be sat in seats they shouldn't be. Shit! That's me! That's us! She might spot Rachel and I impersonating her brother and his fiancée, then shout to the police, 'This man who stuck his hand up his dog's bum outside my house last week is sat in someone else's seat. Throw him out and send him back down south now!'

The shame that will fall upon me in front of thousands! In front of my in-laws. I came in a married man but could walk out separated if she tells Rachel in front of all these people, these 20,000-plus people, that she's seen Pearl and I "doing things." They were completely innocent, explainable things, I hasten to remind you, but it didn't look like that to her or Rainbow Nails Jean. The question is, can I make it through the whole match without her clocking me?

I knew I should've pulled the plug on this whole idea when, on the morning of the match, Rachel told me her dad had found a Bolton shirt for me to wear.

'This wasn't part of the deal,' I complained as I begrudgingly slipped my head through the neck of a Wanderers jersey in my in-laws' living room.

"Awwww," Rachel said, making me pose for a photo.

'No! Not awwwww,' I complained again. 'Errrrrrr. It should be. This feels so wrong.'

'Don't let my dad hear you say that,' she warned me, checking over her shoulder that he didn't hear us from the kitchen where the smell of fried eggs and bacon signalled breakfast was ready.

'Please!' I begged, horrified by what I saw in the living room mirror above the fireplace. 'DO NOT POST THAT PHOTO ON FACE-BOOK.'

It was too late. She'd already done it.

Social media, the whole world, already knew. Me, the lifelong West Ham fan, had committed a cardinal sin and adorned a Bolton shirt. The shield of another team has crossed my heart. I braced myself for the abuse from my friends. I didn't have to wait long.

'*Awful! What have you done to him?*' Moley, one of my closest friends from down south, and a fellow West Ham fan, quickly commented.

When we arrived at the stadium, Rachel was fretting they might not let us in because our faces did not match the photos on the season tickets.

'It'll be fine, babe,' I reassured her.

When we cruised through the turnstiles no-questions-asked and into a packed stadium concourse where we were hit with the smell of beer, hot dogs and piping hot pasties, I was proved right.

All seemed to be going to plan when we took our seats a good half hour before kick off, so Rachel had enough time to locate Lofty the Lion, the club mascot. Doing one better than that, she even managed to catch his eye and exchange waves with him. I suspected this was the only reason she wanted to come, and I thanked my lucky stars she only made me wear a Bolton shirt and not a Lofty the Lion suit. She found it highly amusing when Lofty ran onto the pitch, kicked a ball, fell over and everyone cheered. Seconds later, a chorus of boos rung around the stadium.

'What are they booing for?' Rachel asked.

'The away team just came onto the pitch to warm up,' I said.

'Imagine going to work and getting booed,' Rachel pondered. 'I'd actually cry if I went to school and the kids booed me.'

She had a point! And, I'm in danger of getting booed too, if Mrs Pointer tells the hordes of Bolton fans surrounding me that I'm really a West Ham fan who does the dirty with his dog.

'Talking of school,' Rachel said. 'Funny story from yesterday.'

'What happened?' I asked, trying to blend into the crowd and stay out of Mrs Pointer's sight.

'We were teaching the kids about body parts and asked if they knew any. A five-year-old boy called Olly put his hand up and shouted out "TITS!"'

'How'd you handle that one?' I asked.

'Me and the teacher tried not to laugh, but how can you not?' she said.

When the teams come onto the pitch for the kick-off, the club anthem, "The Wanderer," sounds around the ground. I mumble my way through the verse, then join in with the first chorus.

'Cos I'm a Wanderer. Yes I'm a Wanderer. Going round and round and round and round,' I sing.

Now, there are many things I was sure I'd never do in life – eat a hedgehog (unless it has brown sauce on it. Everything tastes good with brown sauce); dare to tell Rachel her breath smells in the morning; commit blasphemy by singing the song of another football team other than West Ham. Yet here I am doing that last one and having a great time doing so. I feel bad that I'm actually enjoying it but can't stop myself.

Before I know it, I'm also singing along to the catchy numbers, "Oh When the Whites Go Marching In," "White Army!" and, "We Are the One and Only Wanderers." All those songs get a few airings to the rhythm of someone banging a drum as the Bolton fans give heart, soul, song and saliva to become the 12th man and rouse the Bolton players to beat Gillingham's 11. It doesn't work.

Come halftime, Bolton are two goals down and the locals are not looking best pleased. The groundsman isn't forking the divots in the pitch like he was before the game; he's more stabbing at them in anger. Lofty the Lion isn't waving anymore. He's prowling the small section of Gillingham fans for folk he can maul, growling at them. The home fans around me aren't so much munching on their halftime snacks, more chewing over why this always happens to them.

With most of the spectators heading off for halftime refreshments and toilet breaks, I worry that Mrs Pointer will find it easier to see me with all these empty seats around me. I push my cap down over my forehead to try and hide my face as Rachel's dad keeps up a decades-long tradition and spirits up by handing out bags of crisps from a Walker's 12-pack. He might be known down his local church as DJ Disco Dave the Rave, but in row A of the East Stand just behind the dugouts, he's called The Crisp Man. Not wanting to risk being spotted by Mrs Pointer, I politely refuse the crisps and go get a pasty.

Taking the long way around to avoid her, I walk up about 20 steps, across an entire row of empty seats and then down a stairwell manned by another steward.

At a little stall underneath a big telly showing the halftime scores around the country in the stadium concourse, I know I can't afford any mistakes ordering a pasty or my cover may be blown. As simple a task as it may sound, I failed miserably doing so in Chapter 11, "Cold Pie, Warm Pasty". I remember the lesson the lady in Greenhalgh's Bakery taught me that day. Her words of wisdom come to me in a ghostly, echoing voice from the past.

'If you want a meat and potato pasty, you have to actually say, meat and potato pasty. If you just say meat and potato, you'll get a pie.'

I remind myself on approach to the stall that any errors would highlight the fact that I'm not from round here and greatly increase the chances of Mrs Pointer identifying me. The stakes are high. I speak to a young lad wearing Clark Kent-style glasses.

'Meat and potato pasty, please.'

'Here you go,' says Clark Kent as he hands me a pasty so hot in a paper bag that it burns my hands.

Back in my seat and devouring my pasty thinking it's as nice as pie, I feel a mixture of pride and relief. Pride that I can now order a meat and potato pasty with the ease of a local, and relief that I didn't create a scene like last time. That relief is short-lived, however, because as I choke on a hot piece of potato, I see Mrs Pointer move away from her stairwell and trudge up the steps in my direction. I bury my face into my pasty and pray she doesn't see me.

Seconds later, I get a tap on the shoulder.

'Eh, loov. Would you put your cap on t'centre forward's head to make him g'faster? He's like bloomin' cart horse.'

'Hello again!' I say with my mouth full, feigning surprise to see her.

'How's Pearl?' she asks. 'No more toilet trouble?'

'Normal service resumed,' I reply with a nervous laugh, hoping Rachel hasn't overheard so I'll have some explaining to do.

'Fingers crossed this lot can pull their socks up second half,' she says before heading back to her spot in the stairwell. 'See you again, love.'

She must've had her toes crossed, too, because by the end of the game, Bolton battle back and equalise with two goals and fall just short of winning the game at the death.

While they had to settle for a draw, it seems I won a friend. Next morning, when I walk Pearl past Mrs Pointer's house, she gives me a wave from behind her living room window, then comes out the house in her dressing gown.

''Ere you are, love, this one'll meck you go even faster,' she says with a wink, handing me a brand-spanking-new Bolton Wanderers cap.

I wear my new cap to the next two home games. Which they both lose. I've since been declared a bad omen by my father-in-law and banned from going again.

Chapter 24

Rat Man

There are pivotal moments in our lives when we know important change has taken place: at the dawn of puberty when you notice hair growing around your vegetable patch and worry you need to go to hospital; when your partner no longer closes the toilet door when performing and actually wants to talk to you while they download; involuntarily groaning the same noises as your parents when you get up from a chair (oooooooohhhh!).

Another one of those watersheds arrives when I least expect it and is summoned up by the unlikeliest of characters.

It's bedtime on a Monday night and something small, black and hairy has just bolted between my legs and disappeared underneath me while I'm on the toilet.

'AHHHHHH!' I shriek like a baboon burning its arse on a hot car bonnet in a safari park in July. It's the most effeminate noise I've ever made, but I have to admit it, I am PETRIFIED.

I shuffle as fast as I can out of the toilet with my boxers still around my ankles and slam the door closed behind me.

'Do NOT go in there!' I order Rachel who is busy plaiting her hair in our bedroom so it's curly in the morning.

'Oh god,' she complains. 'Not again! Have you sprayed?'

'No, but I have just seen a rat in the bathroom!'

'A what?'

'A rat. A little black one.'

'OH MY GOD! How'd you know it was a rat?'

'Because I've seen *Ratatouille* and know what they look like,' I reply sarcastically. 'It was a rat. Trust me.'

'Errrrr. What are we gonna do?' Rachel panics.

'This,' I declare, pulling the bedroom curtains open and looking to the night sky for his famous lights of salvation, 'is a job for Rat Man.'

Just like citizens in distress used to do in Batman, we wait with anticipation in the house for the arrival of a strapping superhero wearing a cape, an eye mask and underpants over his tights. Surely Rat Man or his sidekick Robin will hear our telepathic cry for help and get here faster than a rat up a drainpipe, right? Wrong. Rat Man must already be in bed because our call is not heeded. Our next move is to phone Bolton Council the next morning. They're very helpful and promise to send their very own Rat Man.

'Graham will be with you tomorrow morning,' they say.

Meantime, we're going to have to keep the upstairs toilet door closed and hope Janice, as we've called the rat, isn't in there using my tea tree mint shower gel to clean her rat tits.

Cometh the next morning, cometh Rat Man.

'You must be Graham,' I say to the little old man in a white bobble hat and a navy blue overall on my doorstep.

'That'd be me,' Graham says, stepping inside, holding a little blue holdall with some tools in it. The zip on his little blue holdall is broken and held together with a couple of safety pins. It looks like he's still using his very first school bag. Hardly the stuff of superheroes. I'm already seriously doubting this man's ability to catch the rat.

Rat Man Graham places his tatty little school bag on the floor in our landing and this is the moment when I imagined he'd put his hands on his hips and say something like, 'So where is the dirty rat?' in a New York accent.

Disappointingly, he does no such thing but does ask a question about my guitar stood on a stand in the living room.

'Do you play?' he asks, pointing at it.

'Only for fun,' I reply.

'I used play back int' day,' he says, adjusting his Covid mask.

'Oh yeah? Wanna know about the rat?' I remind him, brusquely changing the subject to our rodent-related issues. There's no time for idle chatter when Janice could be up there rat-tat-tat-tatting on the drainpipes to call her mates to come join her in our power shower.

'Oh yeah sorry, go on, tell me. What's gone on?' Rat Man asks.

'Two nights ago, I saw a rat run into the bathroom and disappear behind the cistern. I think there's a gap in the toilet casing around the pipes that it's got through somehow.'

'You know,' Graham infers, taking his bobble hat of his head to itch his bald scalp, 'int' winter they like to come inside f'warmth.'

'Really?' My skin begins to crawl off of my skeleton.

'They're nocturnal, too, that's probably why you've seen it at night. 'Ow big's the hole?' he enquires.

'About the size of a 50p, I'd say.'

'Well,' he carries on, 'a rat can get through any gap half its size.'

'Jesus.' I shudder, my arm hairs standing on end.

'And . . .' He's not done yet with the "Did You Know?" intro, '. . . an adult male can run at 15mph,' Graham says.

'Sounds about right. It moved like shit off a shovel,' I say.

'That's why we have to kill 'em with traps and not catch 'em. We wouldn't stand a chance otherwise.'

'I thought as much,' I say. 'My wife asked me, to ask you, if you could pop a glass on it, then put it outside with a piece of paper to spare its life.'

'Oh no. We don't do that, I'm afraid,' he sincerely apologises, thinking I was being serious.

'It's okay. I'll tell her you did though, to make her feel better.'

'Okay-dokey. Mum's the word. Tell you what,' he says, putting on some yellow rubber gloves. 'I'll have a look at your drains and gutters outside first. Then in your bathroom for any residue or droppings. That way we'll know if it's part of a mischief or not.'

'A what?'

'A mischief. That's the name for a pack of rats.'

'Oh. I thought it was called a rat pack,' I joke.

'Well if you hear Frank Sinatra sing-gin' through't pipes, you know who's culprit,' he says.

'I'll keep an ear out for "Rat's Life,"' I say, clapping my hands together, happy that we're finally getting down to rat catching business and I'll soon be able to drop my own droppings in peace again.

'I'll leave you to it,' I say as he goes to check the drains and gutters before toddling up the stairs with his little blue school bag in his right hand.

Fifteen minutes later I hear footsteps coming down the stairs.

'I've left some poison int' hole behind your toilet. We'll come back in two weeks to see what's gone on in there.'

'Thanks so much,' I say.

'Can you just sign this paper to say I've been?' he asks by the front door.

I hope he means he's been to catch the rat and not been to the toilet like the dog groomer.

'Of course,' I say, flaring my nostrils and checking the air for any signs of foul play. Thankfully, I detect only the smell of egg sandwiches from his little blue holdall.

As I sign the pest control papers, Rat Man opens up a new line of conversation. 'So where's that accent from?' he asks.

'Essex. I married a Boltonian and moved up here.'

'Been up 'ere long?'

'Just over a year now.'

'Ah right.'

'We actually came here from Spain,' I say. 'Scariest thing we ever had in the house there was a cockroach.'

'What was it that you were doing there?' he asks.

'My wife and I were professional singers,' I answer.

'I love going gigs, me,' he replies. 'I'll listen to absolutely anything, me.'

Now this is when the Basildon boy, the southerner in me, is beginning to get restless. His little voice in my head starts to nag me.

"Just get that little piece of paper signed so Rat Man can get on with his day and you with yours. He's probably got another job to get to. Crack on sunshine."

But then my more recent Lancastrian social conditioning takes over and a new voice in my head in a northern accent answers back:

"Ask him if he's got time f'brew. He seems like nice bloke. And, you were bloomin' rude earlier on when he asked you about playing guitar and you replied by telling him to get looking f'rat. Just like you were rude to the dog groomer when she wanted to chat with you. Get kettle on and have a natter about music to meck up for it."

'Time for a quick cuppa before you leave?' I ask, heeding my inner Lancastrian's words.

He pulls up an overall sleeve and checks his watch.

'Oh go on then. Why not?'

'Sugar?' I check.

'Two please.'

The Basildon boy in me is raging and goes to sulk on the sofa. 'You've changed, Chermside. And it ain't for the better,' is my southern voice's parting shot.

I place two cups of tea down on the table in my living room overlooking the back garden lawn. A pigeon comes in to raid some seed Rachel left on our bird table.

'Sorry, I've got no biscuits,' I apologise.

'I actually bring me own,' Ratman says before reaching into his little blue school bag to reveal a pack of digestive biscuits he prepared earlier. I officially love this dinky man, his little blue school bag and his personal biscuit supply. I want to take his white bobble hat off and stroke his head, then plait his remaining three hairs. He's a delight.

'Would you like a biscuit?' he offers.

'Love one. Thanks!'

Dunking our digestives, the conversation carries on from where it left off pre-cuppa: music.

'So, you were saying . . .' I prompt him. 'You like going to gigs?'

'Yeah, back int' good 'ole days. I seen 'em all before they were famous; Joy Division. Happy Mondays. New Order. I could go on forever, really . . .'

'Any modern bands you'd like to go see?' I ask.

'I'm hoping to catch Xavier Rudd in Manchester in September.'

'Who?'

'Xavier Rudd. The only way I could describe it,' he says, breaking a digestive in half, deep in thought, 'would be, aboriginal reggae.'

'Love the sound of that,' I say. 'Let's Spotify him.'

Seconds later, Xavier Rudd is playing on shuffle over my phone. While we're sipping on our hot tea and dipping our biscuits on a cold winter morning in Lancashire, we're transcended to the soundscapes of the Australian outback: didgeridoos; the plaintive calls of eagles; spine-tingling aboriginal chants, all laced together by the delicate finger picking of an acoustic guitar and profound, thought-provoking lyrics of activism:

"That government hand, taking blood and land . . . but your warrior spirit lives on and it is strong."

'This song's called "Spirit Bird,"' he informs me, pulling down his mask to bite into a biscuit. 'It's about the indigenous Australians and how they were massacred by the colonial British.'

We keep listening. I'm gripped.

"Soldier on my good countrymen . . . joining hearts and hands in ancestral twine."

The music, the lyrics, the message of struggle and fight and defiance, they give me goosebumps. Freeze my spine. They're beautiful. This is the best thing I've heard in a very long time. I would never have discovered this musical treasure if I'd listened to the southern voice in my head that wanted to kick him out the door as soon as the job was done.

'Thanks so much for this recommendation, Rat Man, I mean, erm, Graham,' I say, raising my teacup.

'Mind if I eat me butty?' he asks, withdrawing some sandwiches from his bag wrapped up in foil.

''Course not.'

'Would you like one?' he offers. 'They're bacon, egg and brown sauce.'

'Thanks very much,' I accept even though I can see the bread is drenched in my least favourite thing ever – butter!

As the playlist moves onto the next song, more socially conscious lyrics sound to some truly reggaesmic rhythms:

"You're spraying your chemical, to increase your decimal, to continue domination, holding people down."

'He's playing in Manchester, you said?' I ask while chewing on my sandwich, thinking that butter in a butty doesn't taste that bad after all.

'September, I think,' he says, rolling his sandwich foil into a ball. 'Well, thanks f'cuppa. Best be off. Rats won't be turning themselves in, sadly.'

As I watch Rat Man walk back up the drive with his schoolbag in one hand ready to go and save more citizens from the perils of invading vermin, I realise important, positive change has taken place. Fifteen months ago when I arrived, I would never have thought to say hello to a stranger, let alone spend half an hour saying a long goodbye over a cup of tea, biscuits and a buttered butty in my very own living room. I love the influence the north is having on me. How it's helping me evolve. I'm becoming more sociable. More open. More human. Less uptight.

And Rat Man, who was full of pleasant surprises, has reminded me of the oldest life lessons: judge a book by its cover and a colourful, life-moulding moment in the black and white drudgery of everyday life may pass you by.

Chapter 25

Grab-a-Cab

Words you hope your taxi driver never says: 'You got those directions in braille?'; 'Look! No hands!'; 'I don't take cash or card.'

Hurtling around the claustrophobic country lanes of deepest, darkest Yorkshire in December, our taxi driver puts the frighteners up Rachel and I with one of his own – 'I'm from a family of drug dealers,' he reveals at the wheel.

This was not what we'd dreamed of on a New Year's Eve we'd planned to go out and celebrate in style. Well, in our rain-soaked ponchos, actually, because Rachel and I are currently walking the Leeds to Liverpool Canal on the final day of 2021.

Coming good with the promise that I made in Fe-bra-rary (see Chapter 15), it's now our fourth day traipsing along the canal spanning the entire width of Northern England. We're about two-thirds of the way to our next stop, Skipton in North Yorkshire, when we realise we're running out of time to arrive at our B&B before the check-in deadline of 7pm. This unusual and annoyingly early check-in cut-off time is due to the extenuating New Year's Eve circumstances.

"We have lives to lead too," the B&B management wrote in the *Fawlty Towers*-style confirmation email. Being beggars for the in-demand accommodation on one of the busiest night of the year, we couldn't be choosers.

Not only are we cutting it fine to arrive at our digs before they close for the night, we're also running the risk of losing an 8pm reservation at an Indian Restaurant.

A first-world problem that last issue may very well be, but tonight means a lot to us. This is the only New Year's Eve in more than a decade we've been able to go out and celebrate. Pre-pandemic, we'd always worked, singing our hearts out for the big build-up to midnight. During these Covid times, all we've been able to do is stay home and watch telly. Next year, we very much hope and expect to be singing for our suppers again. Tonight then, with the world reopened, presents a rare opportunity for us to join in the festivities. Our plan is simple – after a 15-mile walk in the freezing cold and face-slicing rain, we'll fill our faces with curry, then do something we hardly ever do: go out and get royally drunk. We just want to take advantage of this unique chance to join in with the game of life.

Popping into a pub on the canal towpath, we ask the staff if they know any local taxi firms. Luckily they do, and they kindly offer to call us a cab. The good news is, the cab firm says they can pick us up. The bad news? We'll have to wait around an hour because of how busy they already are. We gratefully accept and take advantage of the time we have to wait by ordering some food at a booth in the bar.

'I'll have a bacon butty, please,' I say to a waiter, running my finger up and down the menu. 'With butter, and make the bacon crispy, please.'

'Okay thanks. For you, love?' the waiter says, turning to Rachel.

'I'll have a tuna butty, please.'

'And to drink?' asks the waiter with his tactile pen hovering over a handheld device.

'A pint of Peroni, please,' I answer.

'Same for me, please,' Rachel says.

When the waiter leaves the table, Rachel smiles at me like I'm a toddler that's just wiped for the first time.

'With crispy bacon. AND butter. Really?' she queries.

'When the Rat Man came a few weeks ago, he gave me a buttered butty,' I say, taking off my poncho. 'It was actually alright.'

'And, you just called it a butty, not a sandwich,' she says.

'You lot are starting to rub off on me,' I admit.

'I knew you'd offered Rat Man a brew, but I didn't know you had a buttered butty with him as well,' Rachel says like she's missed out on a game-changing piece of information.

'Now you know,' I say, coming clean.

'Well I never,' she says, slack-jawed. 'You really are becoming one of us.'

Soon after our orders are taken, our beers arrive.

'Here's your pints of pepperoni,' a waitress says.

I splutter a giggle as the pints hit the table.

'What's so funny?' Rachel whispers once she's gone.

'The waitress just said pint of pepperoni.'

'So?'

'The beer's called Peroni, not pepperoni,' I say.

'Oh yeah,' Rachel notes with a chuckle.

Soon after we polish off our pints of pepperoni and butties, we get the call that our taxi has arrived and hop aboard. We'll give the taxi firm a make-believe name to protect their reputation. Let's call them Grab-a-Cab.

We now have just over half an hour until 7pm to make the trip to Skipton that, according to the maps app on my phone, should take around 21 minutes. Plenty of time for Grab-a-Cab to get us there. In theory.

The chatty taxi driver accelerates away with his mouth going as fast as his car – 100mph. We've hardly had time to clip in our seatbelts when he tells us about his prison fodder family.

'Yeah man, most of my tribe have done time or are still doing time,' he says, turning down a drum and bass track threatening to break the speakers.

In the backseat, we both remain silent and stare at his bulging, crazy eyes in the rearview mirror and pray his next words will be about how he broke the family mould.

'Not me though.'

Relief sweeps over us both.

'I'm on the run,' he says with death in his eyes.

We buzz down the windows, unlock the back doors from the out-side and roll out of the cab while it's still moving before tumbling down a ditch to the sound of gunshots.

Were this a Bond film, that's what would've happened. But since it's not, I'll tell you what he really said in his Manchester, Gallagher-brothers-esque accent.

'Not me though. I've made sure not one drug deal has gone down outside my house. Always grafted me stones off, me. You know what I mean?' he says proudly, rolling his shoulders back and puffing his chest out. 'Everyone knows I've got best trainers on Bradford Road.'

I want to ask how he knows he's got the best trainers on Bradford Road but a more important matter has come to my attention – he's going the wrong way.

When he picked us up, the journey time on the maps app my phone to our accommodation said 21 minutes. It's now showing as 25.

'You do know you're going the wrong way?' I say in a polite, yet direct and informative tone.

I present my phone in the mirror from the backseat to show him I'm closely monitoring our progress.

'Nah, nah, we don't need that thing!' he dismisses the information displaying on the screen. 'I've lived around 'ere 20 years, man, I know more than them phones. The shortcuts, you know what I mean? You though, you're not from round 'ere, are yer?' he says.

'Essex,' I answer curtly, thinking I ain't got time for this shit right now. Any delays could see us sleeping on the streets tonight.

'Yeah, down south, thought so. I got family in London, you know. Mega expensive, man. For the price of a parking space down there I can buy an 'ouse up here.'

This is possibly the only thing he's said so far that's made any sense, but I'm careful not to be drawn into this debate on north/south property prices because our journey time is continuing to rise. Twenty-seven minutes now. More time than we have left before our 7pm check-in deadline.

'Are you sure we're going the right way, because it's still saying we're going the wrong way,' I say, showing my phone again.

'Yeah, yeah! The Barn House. I know it. I know it. Trust me,' he says, clipping a thick hedge with his wing mirror on the driver's side as the tyres screech around a tight bend.

Trust him I most certainly don't. He might have the best trainers on Bradford Road, but I can't offer his driving skills any accolades apart from the most likely to make me bring my bacon butty back up.

Rachel is clinging so tightly onto my right leg with her left hand, her nails are digging into my thigh. I remove them one by one, wincing as I do. Last time I was in this much pain it was because I got a ready salted crisp stuck in a cold sore on my bottom lip. Next time you need to torture someone to get them talking, put a salty crispy in their cold sore. That's a fresh hell no human can stand. FBI – you're welcome!

Without warning, the Grab-a-Cab driver hits the brakes hard on a country lane, reverses, then takes a right down a gravel track where, up ahead, his lights pick out a big barn with a glass façade and thatched roof.

'This is it,' he says, pulling up the handbrake.

'This is definitely not it,' I disagree. 'It's in Skipton, this is not Skipton.'

'You said The Barn House though, right?'

'Yes, The Barn House. In Skipton,' I repeat. 'This isn't Skipton. It's a field.' I follow his confused eyes in the rearview mirror. They roll with regret and self-annoyance when the penny finally drops.

'Don't worry,' he says, hurriedly swinging the car into a three-point turn with the gravel crunching under his tyres. 'I'll take you to Skipton now. You won't pay no more. You've got me word.'

Twenty-odd minutes later, true to his word, the taxi driver with the best trainers on Bradford Road and worst listening skills drops us at our bed and breakfast in Skipton, not charging us a penny more. To make up for his mistake, he very kindly waits until we're inside before leaving.

I buzz the intercom on the front door and our B&B owner opens the door, looking unimpressed we've turned up nearly half an hour late. He scowls at us like two kids late for class.

'I'm Carlos, the owner,' he says coldly. 'Follow me upstairs.'

The crazy cab driver and his award-winning trainers waves us good-bye.

'Appy New Year, yeah,' he shouts out the window before speeding off with his drum and bass music back playing at full volume.

Up on the middle of the B&B's three floors, Carlos shows us into our double room, complete with an en suite bathroom, and gives us the lowdown.

'So, thee eh-Sky Box should work,' he says in heavily accented English, clicking some buttons on a remote. 'That is, of course, if no one's been messing.'

The Sky Box he's pointing the remote at nor the TV responds.

'Do, do do, do do,' he mumbles nervously, pushing the remote buttons a bit harder as if doing so will increase the chances of the Sky Box working.

'Nice place you've got here, Carlos,' I say, filling the awkward silence while we all stare at the blank screen.

'Thanks,' he says pushing the buttons on the remote again. 'It's nicer when no one's been messing with the television. Do, do do, do do . . .'

'We don't really need Sky TV,' I say. 'Normal TV will do us.'

'I don't believe it,' he says, gritting his teeth. 'Someone has been messing. *¡Hijo puta!*'

He doesn't know that I speak Spanish and that I also know he just lost his shit and said "son of a bitch" in his mother tongue.

'It's no big deal, honestly. We can live without it,' I say, trying to play it down. 'Long as we can get the radiators on to warm up, we'll be as good as gold.'

He sulks his way over to the radiators underneath the windows looking out over the car park below, crouches down and starts turning the dials.

'You just turn them to the right to switch them on,' he says. 'Unless of course, someone's been messing,' he repeats while we wait for the radiators to fire up. 'Do, do do, do do . . .' he mumbles, drumming his fingers on his jeans pocket.

I really wish he did, did did, did didn't, do, do do, do do that while he waits for stuff to start working. It's making me nervous.

'I don't believe it,' he growls again. 'Someone's been messing with these as well.'

Down on one knee, wobbling the radiator's dials to try and spark them into life, he looks again at his watch. He then tuts and glowers at us like it's all our fault they're not working.

'Okay,' he says, standing up. 'I have to go out now. But leave it with me. I'll get maintenance to come have a look at the radiators.'

He unzips a coat pocket, pulls out his phone and sends a voice note to his maintenance man. 'Sorry, Brian, I know, it's late, but can you make me a favour? Can you come and look at the radiators in room four? Looks like someone's been messing with them.'

He then scratches his head and stares at us deep in thought. 'Do, do do, do do,' he mumbles out the side of his mouth.

'Come on and do the conga,' I want to say.

'As for the TV,' he says. 'Fingers crossed the eh-Sky Box just needs rebooting. I'll do that now.'

Before leaving, he has some parting words of advice.

'Oh! Before I forget!' he says, holding the door to our room half-open. 'Some teeps and treeks.'

Now, I'm assuming he means tips and tricks about Skipton. Some inside information about things to do and places to go around town. I'm very wrong.

'Firstly, when you use the toilet at night, don't close the door. Just put the door to the frame without actually closing it. Like they are key-sing. This way you do not wake up the people above or below.'

I relay back to him what he's just said to show I've understood. 'Don't actually close the toilet door, kiss the frame with it.'

'Correct. Also,' he says, 'there is a leetle window in the bathroom. Please keep it open to let the smells out.'

'Gotcha!' I say, thumbs up. 'Window open. Smells out.'

'And, last teep and treek. When you unlock your door from the outside. Put the key in, pull it out a leetle, then wiggle it a leetle. Then it should open okay. Please don't bang or shake the door. This will wake up the people above and below.'

'Put it in. Pull it out. Wiggle it. No banging,' I paraphrase.

He then wishes us a half-hearted happy New Year and closes the door behind him.

'You get all that?' I say to Rachel who collapses onto the bed exhausted after our long day hiking in the cold.

'Manuel, Carlos, whatever his name is. He can do one with his tips and tricks if we're not getting what we pay for,' she says, untying her laces on her walking boots.

Despite this far from ideal start to our stay, all is not lost. We can live without Sky TV and since we're planning to go out, neither are the cold radiators that important. All we need is a hot shower to warm up and freshen up from the eight hours we've spent walking in the cold and we'll be ready for that night out on the tiles we'd promised ourselves.

Trouble is, there's no hot water either. We run the hot tap for a good few minutes but the water remains arctic.

'I can't go to a restaurant like this,' Rachels says, getting up from the bed and looking her dishevelled, tired and wind-battered self up and down in the mirror. 'I look like nobody owns me.'

We reluctantly accept that we have no other option than to cancel the 8pm dinner reservation while we wait for maintenance man Brian to arrive. When he does, around 9pm, he's successful at getting the Sky Box working, but he's not able to get the heating or hot water fired up. He apologises profusely, advises us to speak to Carlos to discuss some form of compensation, and brings up a load of extra blankets.

As we insulate the bed with the extra layers, Rachel has a flick through the Sky channels.

'There's a *Royle Family* marathon on all night,' she beams, jumping into bed to warm up.

'Plan B, it is!' I say, then run into town to buy a couple of beers and a falafel kebab each.

Back in the room, we make the best of what we've got and have a cosy night under the covers with Manchester's funniest fictional family.

Waking up on New Year's Day with no hangover, feeling as fresh as the Best Trainers on Bradford Road, we thank our lucky stars that someone up there was messing with our plans. A night in laughing our heads off with the Royle family was so much better than a night out getting royally drunk. Sometimes, life happens for you, not to you.

Chapter 26

Can't Bop, Won't Bop

'Can you bop?' Rachel's grandad asks me.

'Eh?' I reply, cupping my ear to hear him better over the loud disco music.

'Can you,' he repeats, pointing at me and leaning in closer from his chair by my side, 'bop?' He wiggles his hips and does a seated twist.

'What do you mean, Stanley?'

'Can you dance? I love a dance, me.'

'Erm . . . bopping's not really my thing,' I say, holding onto my chair for dear life with both hands so he can't drag me onto the dance floor in the function suite of the hotel we're staying in.

Due to Covid restrictions, I've had to wait a long time to see Rachel's dad work his magic as DJ Disco Dave the Rave. But now that wait is over because, ladies and genitals, the British Prime Minister has let DJ Disco Dave the Rave loose again and he's on tour! Yes, you heard me right, on a bloody tour! Armed with his thousands-strong CD collection (he outright refuses to update his rig and use any form of music streaming platform. He calls it "cheating"), he's playing two nights at a hotel in Lytham St Annes.

Being the man of the hour, DJ Disco Dave the Rave has not only given Rachel and I free tickets to the second and final night of his weekend tour, he's also scored us lodgings for free. It's the hotel's way of thanking him for the army of line dancers that he's brought with him from his church's congregation. DJ Disco Dave the Rave and his line dancing disciples are big business!

'There is a catch,' Rachel informed me in front of the telly one evening a few days before the big night.

'Go on.'

'The party is fancy dress.'

'I should've guessed already,' I sighed. 'Who are we going as?'

'Homer and Marge Simpson,' Rachel said, unveiling a tall blue wig for herself and a yellow swimming hat that I'll have to squeeze my head into to depict Homer's huge bald head.

I'm really not a fan of fancy dress. In fact, I'm not a fan of any dress at all. I'd walk the streets in my birthday suit if I could just because not having to decide what clothes to wear is one less decision to make every day in a life full of difficult decisions.

'Can I say no?' I asked, already knowing the answer.

'Well, you can. But everyone will think you're boring and you'll be the only one.'

'Point taken,' I conceded, noting with dread the yellow face paint on the coffee table with which I'll have to colour my face.

'Dad is going as Mrs Brown,' she said, inflicting the end of her sentence with eyebrows aloft like this is good news.

'Who?'

'Mrs Brown. From *Mrs. Brown's Boys.*'

'Doh!' I grumble, knowing there's no way I can wriggle my way out of this if DJ Disco Dave the Rave is going in fancy dress, too.

When Saturday night at the Line Dancing Party comes, I discover a whole new unimagined world.

Walking into the function suite of the seaside hotel, I see all manner of fancy dress characters hot stepping to country and western rhythms; a group of five grannies dressed as the Spice Girls calling themselves the Nice Girls; a gang of morris dancers, all braces, hats and tassels; and couples dressed as famous duos – Super Mario and Luigi; Batman and Robin; Laurel and Hardy.

Rachel's grandad Stanley, who's in school uniform, is sat at a table reserved for us looking out across the dance floor. Before I can take my seat, I'm collared into running a few errands. Some morris dancing ladies with Welsh accents ask if I can help them pin their country's flag up. I happily oblige, jump on a chair, and pin it to a white curtain running along a ceiling rail by their table partitioning the large hall. They can't thank me enough for doing so.

Then a pair of the Nice Girls, who see me in flag-raising action, ask if I can do the same for them with their Lancashire flag. Again, I do as I'm asked with pleasure and pin up their famous red rose next to their table.

So this is why I was invited! I'm the flag putter upper for my father-in-law who has the biggest heart but very small legs at five foot four inches tall. All makes sense now. I'm here to do the jobs he can't.

Speaking of the devil, there he is, dressed up as Mrs Brown in a curly brown wig, beige cardigan, and flowery, ankle-length frock on a raised stage, banging out hit after country hit. He has almost everybody in the room up line dancing on a packed dance floor. They're all thumbs in belt buckles; sliding sideways and back; shaking hips; pivoting on pigeon-toe tips; unleashing long-leg kicks. It's lovely to see people enjoying themselves again, after nearly two years of enduring Covid restrictions.

'You've not had a dance yet,' one of the Nice Girls accuses, standing over me in my chair. She has "Old Spice" written on a name badge on her chest.

'I wouldn't know how to,' I say. 'I'm watching and learning.'

'You can't koom in 'ere without avin' a dance,' Old Spice warns.

'I might do later,' I reply, nervously shuffling in my seat, knowing full well that I won't be dancing upon any circumstances.

As much as I'm probably more comfortable on stage singing than I am walking down the street, dancing is completely outside of my comfort zone. It's not something I do, plan to start doing or, indeed, have ever done. Were they to make a programme about people like me, they'd call it, *Can't Bop, Won't Bop.*

I cling onto my chair a bit tighter and watch Rachel and her grandad bop to "Achy Breaky Heart" by Billy Ray Cyrus together.

When the song finishes, they both come sit down next to me because big things are about to happen: DJ Disco Dave the Rave is about to set the night alight by unleashing the event everyone's been eagerly awaiting – the Stand Up Bingo!

Now, you might want to sit down for this because you wouldn't believe how it ends – Rachel is the last one left standing and wins the bingo. She snares a bottle of red and white wine and a giant block of Cadbury's Dairy Milk as big as a park bench. The full house cries foul play.

'Fix! Rigged! Swindle!' they jeer playfully.

Rachel, because she's kind and thoughtful and not because she bows to the pressure of the nepotism accusations, gifts the wine and chocolate to a lady called Ivy who's dressed as a giant inflatable boob.

Before getting the party re-started, Rachel's dad has a few more words to say. In his Mrs Brown get-up, he addresses the function suite full of his fancy dress disciples. They fall silent and hang on their musical messiah's every word.

'So, er . . . what a turn out,' Mrs Brown starts off, replacing his fancy dress glasses with reading specs on the raised stage at the front of the room.

'It's been quite a while since we've been able to do this, so it's great to see you all,' Rachel's dad says, reading from notes he's scribbled on a tatty piece of paper. The room cheers and applauds in agreement.

'Sadly, since we were last 'ere, we've lost a few people. Bloomin' good'uns n' all,' he regrets. 'Rose, Doug, Shirley. We hope you're up there in heaven 'avin' a dance with us.'

Cue more applause and a few "aww's."

'Our thoughts are also with Grace who was sadly blue-lighted to hospital last night.'

'Here, here,' echoes around the room.

'Now, we do appreciate that the disco might go on quite late for some of you. So, if you do slip off during the night, we will miss you,' Rachel's dad says.

'Sounds like he's killing the rest of 'em off!' I say to Rachel.

'Now,' he announces with a change of tone and demeanour that suggests he's got some happier news. 'We've got a nice surprise for you all . . .'

'Ooooh,' the room responds excitedly in unison.

'Because I know you're probably all sick of listening to my rubbish . . .'

'You must be a mind reader,' heckles a man dressed as a bottle of hand sanitiser who's got the words "Pump Me Hard" written across his chest.

'Ha, bloody, ha,' Rachel's dad replies. 'Now where were I? Please. Turn. Over,' he reads aloud from the bottom of the page. 'Oops sorry, I wasn't supposed to read that bit. It's your fault,' he says, pointing at the hand sanitiser man. 'You made me lose me train of thought, you. So as I were about to say . . . I've got two special guest tribute acts doing a turn each for you all tonight.'

'Doing a turn?' I quiz Rachel. 'What does that mean?'

'Some singers are going to do a set each.'

'Ooooh.'

'We've got Shania Twain coming on later,' he announces. 'And, we've got Barry White doing a turn for you too, any minute now.'

'He's got some connections, your dad, hasn't he?' I whisper, leaning into Rachel.

'What's 'appening?' Rachel's grandad asks, fiddling with his hearing aid.

'Barry White coming on,' Rachel says directly into his right ear.

'There's a fight going on?' he says, looking around the room. 'Where?'

'No. No one's fighting, Grandad. Barry! Barry White! He's singing 'ere tonight.'

Minutes later, up on the stage now vacated by Rachel's dad, there's a Barry White tribute kicking off his turn to "My First, My Last, My Everything." Queues at the bar re-form and people get up from their seats to have a boogie with Barry.

Rachel's grandad Stanley stays sat at the table to have a chat with us.

'Did you have the tea?' he asks.

'No,' Rachel says. 'We got here too late.'

'They were nowt' of it. It were more like a meal f'sparrows in me back garden,' he complains. 'It's the same every year here wit' food. They're as tight as a fish's backside. And that's watertight.'

'You are funny,' Rachel says.

'Did your Dad tell you that I saw your nan last week?' he says, switching to matters more poignant.

'No, he didn't,' Rachel says, leaning in and keen to know more.

'Yeah I did. I saw your nan at bottom of me bed int' middle o' night. Clear as day, large as life. Like she were still alive.'

'Did she say anything?' Rachel, who dearly misses her late nan Stella, asks.

'No. She were just there with me. It were nice.'

Rachel gives him a comforting rub on the forearm.

'Fifty-eight years we were married, you know? We didn't spend a single night apart. Never. It's bloomin 'ard,' Stanley says, palming a tear off his cheek.

'Let's go get a drink, shall we, Grandad?' Rachel says, trying to cheer him up.

By the time they're back from the bar, Barry White has finished his turn and Shania Twain has taken to the stage.

'You're still the one I run to, the one that I belong too-hoo-hoo,' she sings in a cowgirl hat, spurred boots and a big buckled belt.

'Is that Barry White?' Stanley asks, pointing at the cowgirl.

'No, Grandad. He's been and gone. That's Shania Twain,' Rachel says, getting him up to speed.

'Who?'

'Shania. Twain. Shania Twain.'

'What's she hired?' he asks, looking confused while adjusting his hearing aid to the increasing noise level in the room.

'Nothing. That's the second singer. She's called, Shania. Twain. We need get your specs checked.'

'Oh, I can't keep up, me! All this noise is breaking me deaf aids,' Stanley says, chuckling at himself.

For the final song of Shania's turn, Mamma Maria – as I call my mother-in-law, who's disguised as Mrs Brown's chavy son in a tracksuit and cap – comes over and grabs me by the arm.

'Come and 'ave' a dance, you,' she orders.

'Noooooo,' I plead, just cringing at the thought. I sink into my chair, hoping it will swallow me up and make me disappear.

'Like she just said,' Maria says, pointing at Shania Twain, 'that don't impress me much.'

Kicking and screaming and crying inside, I reluctantly grab onto Mamma Maria's outstretched hand and follow her even though I'd rather stub a toe on a bedpost set in broken glass than get up and dance.

When the song finishes and Shania exits the stage, I try to go sit back down in the comfort and safety of my chair but can't because I'm approached by the same Old Spice who spoke to me earlier in the night.

'Come 'ave a dance with us,' she says, on my case again.

'No, I'm okay, really. I don't even know this song,' I beg, making my excuses.

'Come oooon,' Old Spice insists, refusing to take no for an answer. 'We'll teach you the steps!'

Before I know it, I've got all five Nice Girls – Old Spice, Sloshed Spice, Hairy Spice, Naughty Spice and Sugar and Spice – shouting instructions at me for a dance called The Electric Slide.

'Step right, left together. Step left, right together. Back right, left together,' they yell me through it over the music.

Try as I might, I just can't sort my feet out to follow their simple instructions. My attempt at The Electric Slide is more like geriatric shuffle. At the end of the song, with my yellow Homer Simpson face paint running down my sweaty face, the Nice Girls give me a generous applause.

Stanley compliments me, too. 'See. You can bop,' he says when I exit the dance floor and sit back down next to him.

Old Spice comes over to congratulate me personally. 'Well done, love,' she says.

'I'm a really bad dancer, but I can sing a bit,' I say.

'What, int' shower?' she taunts.

'I actually sang for a living before the pandemic,' I say.

'Did you really?'

'I know you wouldn't think it from my dancing. But I do have some musical bones in my body.'

'Well, that's handy because we need someone to do a turn for us at a fundraiser for Bolton Hospice. Could you do it?' she asks.

'Erm, yeah, of course,' I say, caught off guard without thinking through the finer details.

'You should come along to line dancing on Wednesday nights when you can for rehearsals.'

'Rehearsals?' I panic.

'Yeah. Rehearsals. You'll have to sing a few songs with us as part of your turn.'

And that is how I went from never dancing, to line dancing with Rachel and the Nice Girls on Wednesday nights. Another thing, just like wearing the shirt of a northern football team, that I thought I'd never do.

At the benefit gig for Bolton Hospice organised by Rachel's mum and dad and the line dancers, Rachel and I both do a turn each and help to raise 2,410 quid.

The song and dance was well worth it!

Chapter 27

The Two Ronnies

It's just gone 1am when a metallic silver BMW with blacked-out windows, alloy wheels and a spoiler pops open its boot. It looks like the kind of car a drug dealer, mafia member or man wearing the Best Trainers on Bradford Road would drive.

I wonder what the hell's going on? Who could be at the wheel? What's it doing here with its boot popped open at a time of night when I'm normally dribbling onto my pillow and dreaming of having flying lessons from the blonde in the pop group, Steps? (I hated their music but loved the blonde, Faye. If I hadn't married Rachel, I'd have done it in the cockpit. Asked her to marry me, not erm, it).

The mystery driver stays in the car but the boot remains unusually open. The next step I take, the next move I make, the next thing I do do do, da da da (sorry, I've just heard The Police on the radio), is one I'm about to regret. I should've heeded the warning signs earlier in the day when talked turned to gangsters . . .

***

I'm at my brother-in-law's wedding and the photographer, who I've noticed has a bogey nestled on a long protruding nose hair, is rounding up the guests for the official photos. Damo, one of the groomsmen who I've never met before, comes over to break the ice. He's got the height and hairline of Danny DeVito but sounds like Peter Kay the comedian.

'You talk like the two Ronnies,' he says, sitting down next to me on a wooden picnic bench in the sunny courtyard of the countryside wedding venue.

'Who? The speccy lads from the telly, Corbett and Barker?' I reply.

'No, not them,' he says, throwing his head back, laughing and pointing at me. 'The Ronnie Kray twins.'

'That's Ronnie and Reggie. They're not both called Ronnie,' I correct him, thinking I should be the one pointing and laughing since he's made the mistake, not me.

'Ronnie. Reggie. Whatever they're called. You sound like them. Proper cockney geezer,' he says, poking fun at me, then stands up and breaks into a very bad impression of a cockney swagger. He looks like one of those giant, inflatable stick men you see maniacally throwing their limbs around in second-hand car forecourts.

'I bet they're all like you,' he says, standing over me, not quite finished with the goading. 'Soft, shandy-drinking southerners.'

'I've been up here long enough now to handle it with you boys,' I foolishly reply.

'Have a shot with me then,' he challenges as the wedding photographer and his bogey shout for the bride's nearest and dearest to gather for a shot.

I look at my West Ham watch and balk. It's just gone two in the afternoon.

'No chance, Damo,' I say, winding my neck right back in from where it came. 'I'll be in bed before tea if I do.'

'Come oooon,' Damo says, egging me on and doing up a button on his double breasted tartan waistcoat. 'You said you're one of us. If you are, you'll have a drink with me now. I've been on it since this morning,' he boasts.

I'm not sure what's more worrying. The fact that I just spoke northern and called dinner "tea" again just like I did in Chapter 18 on the evening I met the coin tosser, or the crazy words that are about to come out of my mouth.

'Get the shots in!' I say, accepting his challenge.

Though I seldom drink anything more than one or two beers a week, I'm confident one shot in the middle of the day won't kill me.

Damo, to my horror, after heeding the photographer's call, comes back with two sambucas each.

'Go big or go home,' he says after slamming down shot number two on the picnic bench.

I puff my cheeks out to psyche myself up and reluctantly follow suit. First sambuca – yuck! Second – pass the sick bowl!

I immediately reach for the bottled water I was already drinking to wash away the lingering taste of anise.

'The night is young,' Damo declares with a glint of mischief in his eye (he actually has two eyes but the left one was more mischievous).

If my mum were here, she'd definitely tell me I wasn't allowed to play out with him.

Whilst I sit on the picnic bench swishing water around my mouth, Rachel's grandad takes a seat next to me in the space Damo has just vacated. As always, he has something interesting to say.

''Ere,' he says, poking me in the arm. 'Did you know I were ont' telly a while back.'

'Oh yeah?' I say, popping in a chewing gum to freshen up my sambuca breath. 'Was it at a Bolton match again? We've seen you loads of times on the highlights in your bright yellow jacket on the halfway line.'

'No. It were bloomin' BBC News,' Stanley says.

'Really?'

'Yeah. Couldn't believe me eyes. You know int' lockdown?' he says.

I nod my head to show I'm all ears.

'There were lovely, young couple fetching food for old buggers like me,' he says.

'That was nice of them.'

'Yeah it were. One day. There were ring at door-wah. I opens it and there at end o' drive were loada' cameras and a bag of tattie ash on me doorstep.'

'BBC, you said?'

'Yeah. BBC North West, they said they were from,' Stanley confirms.

'Shall I see if I can find it on t'internet?' I suggest.

Whatever next? First I call dinner "tea" – again! – and now the internet, t'internet? Must be the shots loosening my tongue for that last one. As for that first slip of the northern tongue, I have no excuses.

'Can you see that there? On your phone?' Stanley asks.

'Might be able to. Let's have a look,' I say.

Sure enough, as I get trawling the net, there he is, large as life, in a video clip on BBC North West's website. First on camera is a reporter grilling the considerate couple about why they decided to help out the needy in their neighbourhood.

'It's just what you do, int'it?' the smiling, unassuming man says, linking arms with his wife. 'Help out folk int' need.'

The footage then cuts to the couple placing a carrier bag on Stanley's doorstep, ringing the bell, then walking off to a safe social distance. Seconds later, Rachel's grandad appears, then clocks the television cameras.

'Waheeeyy,' Stanley shouts to the camera, waving with both hands. Clocking the carrier bags at his feet on his doorstep, he asks, 'What's this, 'ere?'

'Some tattie ash we've made for you,' says the generous man now at the end of Stanley's driveway.

'For me?' Stanley checks.

'Yeah, we thought you might like some,' the woman in the couple says.

'Ta' very much,' Stanley says, scooping up the carrier bags.

It's only a nine-second cameo, but we can now proudly say Stanley Lee, As Seen On BBC TV.

'Tell you what, Stanley, since you're now famous, I'll buy you a drink,' I say.

'Ta' very much. I'll 'ave a pint o' Guinness if it's not too much trouble, please.'

'Nothing's too much trouble for you, Stanley,' I say, standing up from our picnic bench and patting him on the shoulder.

'Will you have one with me?' he asks.

'Eh?' I panic, thinking I can't have another drink so soon after two venomous sambucas.

'Go on, 'ave a pint with me,' Stanley says, twisting my arm.

'Oh go on then,' I cave in. I just couldn't say no to an offer to drink a pint with Stanley.

'Back in a sec,' I say before soon returning with two pints of Guinness.

Damo soon makes a reappearance, laughing and pointing at me sipping a pint with Stanley.

'I can see this is gonna get messy,' he says, rubbing his hands together. 'Shandy-drinking southerner, mixing wit' big northern boys.'

'Messy for you, you norvern munk-eeeee,' I fire back with sambuca- and Guinness-fuelled Dutch courage in as broad a cockney accent as I can muster.

Aside from my in-laws, I hardly know most of the wedding guests but everyone is so chatty, friendly and approachable that I can hardly walk two steps without stopping to have a conversation and someone offering to buy me a drink. I successfully and wisely deflect all further offers of alcohol.

Come the meal and the speeches in the function room where all the tables and chairs are decked out in Bolton Wanderers' colours of white and black, a waitress stands over me with red and white wine bottles ready to fill my glasses.

'No thanks, love,' I say. 'Just a jug of water please, when you get the chance.'

Love? Love? Where did that come from? First I say "tea," then "t'internet," and now call someone "love"? Drinking two shots and a pint in a few hours is clearly making me talk like "I am from round here."

That's now the end of the drinking, I tell myself as I chug a glass of water in an attempt to sober up and talk proper again.

Damo, however, has other, very bad ideas. Soon as the speeches and meal are over, he places another sambuca in front of me on the table. I know I should say thanks but no thanks. Eat humble pie for dessert and admit that I'm way out of my depth and that I can't drink with the big northern boys. But, I begin to take Damo's drinking challenge as something of a compliment. A privilege. One of the groomsmen, a VIP wedding guest, wants to have a drink with little old anonymous me. One of our greatest needs as humans is to connect with the members of our tribe. This guy is at the top of my northern tribe. Big Chief Damo wants to teach little chief Chermside from the south lands "how we do things around here." It's like Bear Grylls, the king of piss drinking, inviting me to drink a pot of my own piss with him. I feel honoured. Making this connection feels like progress for me. Like I'm finally fitting in.

I neck the shot, then scoff, 'That all you got?'

'Plenty more where that came from,' Damo says, smelling southern blood.

After the first dance and the cake cutting, the band starts to play and the dance floor fills. It's at this point that I realise that I am definitely under the influence (Damo's very bad one) because, totally out of character, I head straight for the dance floor without any peer pressure whatsoever from line dancing grannies. With sambuca and Guinness fizzing through my veins, I'm moving to the music, liberated from my usual inhibitions and reservations about dancing. I feel like John Travolta even if I may be wiggling my tall, skinny and spindly frame like Mr Bean. Great way to sweat out the alcohol, I tell myself as the band plays "Uptown Funk."

'Uptown funk you up, Uptown funk you up,' the singer belts.

Stepping in time to the music with Rachel and I, Stanley shouts into my ears, 'What's 'e sing-gin'? Funky pump?'

'No, "Uptown funk you up",' I shout back.

'I thought 'e were saying funky pump,' Stanley shouts back. 'I were gonna say – sounds naughty.'

While getting our funky pump on with Rachel and Stanley, I have a flashback to being at a family wedding in my late teens back down south. I remember looking around the room and seeing an empty dance floor and long thunder faces sat around the tables. I got the impression everyone was waiting for an acceptable hour when they could make their excuses for having to leave. I remember thinking that this isn't how it should be. Why was everyone so miserable? Why was everyone so cold? Why was no one talking to each other or having a good time? Yet, as I look around me here, all I can see and think is the opposite. That this is exactly how it should be. People are smiling, chatting and laughing. Dancing, singing and rejoicing. I know it's probably the alcohol talking here but... Love Is in the Air. Love is All Around Me. I Can't Help Falling in Love with all (what do you mean that's plagiarism?) these lovely people that have adopted me as one of their family and friends. They all treat me like one of their own and I've never ever had this sense of belonging before.

As the band moves into a James Brown number, I have a realisation that the north is the place I've been looking for all my adult life. That I'd swap the warmth of Tenerife for the warmth of the people up north all day long. The realisation is moving and I have to choke back tears of drunken happiness. 'I fucking love you all,' I want to shout in everyone's faces as I choke back tears of drunken happiness. Hmmm, salty!

I soon have to choke on more shots, too, because Damo has recruited the help of the best man, Diggers, and my brother-in-law, Danny, to make me drink more.

'You gonna buy me a shot on my wedding day?' Danny shouts into my ears on the dance floor, deploying the emotional blackmail tactic.

'Be rude not to,' I shout back over the band as I'm shaking my money maker to James Brown's lyrics, "Shake your money maker, shake your money maker."

I walk over to the bar past the photographer who's bogey is boogieing to James Brown as he snaps away on the dance floor. My arm is soon twisted into drinking not one more shot but three more by the groom and his VIPs. VIPs now standing for Very Inebriated People. Danny insists I have one with him. So does Damo. So does the best man, Diggers.

This is the moment when, looking back, I should've done a disappearing act. Made a sharp exit like a lone traveller in the middle seat of a plane who's got a fart brewing. But, in my increasingly inebriated state and no longer thinking straight, I say something stupid that only pokes the bears.

'Lightweights, the lot of you,' I sneer, licking a shot glass clean to get every last bit of sambuca residue.

'Fighting talk,' Damo says, slamming a shot glass down on the bar. 'I like it.'

'Another round of doubles,' my brother-in-law shouts to a young barman who looks genuinely worried for me.

Rachel, seeing me, a lightweight perilously punching with the heavyweights, comes over from the dance floor to check on me.

'You okay, baba?' she checks.

'Never been better,' I hiccup.

She insists I drink some of her water.

'Thanks, babe,' I say, draining every last drop like a marathon runner at a water station. 'I needed that.'

The rest of the night plays out with the groom's VIPs grooming me into drinking more and more, despite my best efforts to hide among the guests on the dance floor and stay out of harm's way. At one point I spot them at the bar making Rachel's grandad, complete with fairy lights on his head, drink a Jagerbomb with them. Their appetite for destruction knows no bounds and spares no one.

When the band stops playing around 1am, I feel surprisingly okay. Definitely punch-drunk but not on the ropes. I'm still seeing single, not double. My speech is not slurred. I haven't told anyone I love them, even though I really wanted to. I'm pretty sure I haven't been repeating myself, either. Oh, and I haven't told anyone I love them when I actually fucking love everyone here. Oh shit, I just repeated myself, didn't I? Anyway, I reckon I can probably have just the one more. For the road and all that.

'Nightcap, Damo?' I suggest back at the bar as the band packs up.

'Make it a double,' he says as last orders are called.

Another double blow dealt to my liver, I say goodnight to Damo and leave the bar congratulating myself.

'I did it! I held my own with the big northern boys,' I say to Rachel as we walk back to our room past the venue's vast car park. It's then that we see the boot of the high-spec, flashy BMW pop open.

'Wonder who that is?' Rachel ponders as we link arms.

'That car was here when we arrived this morning,' I do well to remember in my inebriated state. 'Could be one of the wedding guests because it hasn't moved all day.'

'Bit weird how the boot is just left open like that,' Rachel suspects, assuming the role of detective.

Then the driver's window whirs down and the driver leans out and shouts, 'Oi! Two Ronnies. Something int' boot for you.'

'Shit, it's Damo,' I say. 'I hope he's not gonna make me drink more.'

'Just ignore him and come to bed,' Rachel sensibly suggests.

Not wanting to disappoint a master member of the wedding tribe and ruin the hard work I'd put into being accepted into the clan, I reluctantly heed Damo's call.

'You carry on, babe,' I say to Rachel. 'I'll catch you up.'

'Don't be long,' she says. 'And don't drink anymore.'

I give her the thumbs up, then walk over to the boot of the BMW. Inside is a cask of expensive whisky bottles and an array of shiny shot glasses in a wooden case. A kind of "Car Bar," if you will.

Damo exits the driver's seat and we're soon joined by the groom and best man. Once again I consider myself lucky to be included among this select group of the wedding VIPs. I just wish Damo had a flask of peppermint tea and ginger biscuits in the boot to share instead of whisky.

Handing me a glass, Damo asks which whisky I prefer. I plump for Jack Daniels and sip at it neat for the next half hour as we drink, chat and laugh, standing around the boot of Damo's car. For a moment it feels like the perfect end to a perfect day. I've had fun. I've made friends, felt like one of the family. Felt like I've finally found the home I've been searching for all adult life. Best of all, I've seen my brother-in-law marry an amazing, lovely and beautiful lady called Samantha.

But then it all goes south. My head starts to spin, I become light-headed and a tsunami of nauseous shivers washes over my whole body. Sensing very bad things are about to happen, I hit the floor and projectile vomit on all fours down a grassy bank to the rear of the car. It gushes out of my mouth like dragon fire. For a very, very long time.

'That's it, Two Ronnies,' Damo says menacingly. 'Let it all out you soft, southern shandy-drinker.'

Rachel's brother sends her a message that I'm in a mess and in need. She comes to the rescue in her cow onesie with a bottle of water and a packet of tissues.

'What have you done to him, you nasty pasty?' she shouts at Damo.

'Just teaching him a lesson,' Damo laughs.

'I'll teach you a lesson,' she warns him. 'Stop making him drink.'

'Sorry, babe. I just wanted to be sociable,' I apologise while sobbing like a drunken fool.

Worse for wear, I clamber to my feet, bile dripping from my mouth, vomit all over my wedding suit, eyes streaming from the deep-throated retching. Damo tries his luck again.

'Shot?' he offers, holding out a bottle of Jameson's.

'In the words of *The Two Ronnies*, Damo, it's good night from me,' I slur.

Chapter 28

Happy Humping Ground

It's Monday morning and 36 hours since my insides spilled out of my mouth at my brother-in-law's wedding. I've found my stomach and lungs and plugged them back in, but my liver has moved back in with its parents after what I did to it, refusing to come home. I'm still feeling very fragile as I patiently wait behind a woman at the counter in the post office.

'I've got irritable bowel, y'see,' says a woman in jeans, a pink anorak and a white bobble hat to the post office clerk. 'The north wind's always blowing for me. Some days it's like a gay force wind.'

'A what, love?' asks the woman behind the counter.

'A gay force wind. Like it's gonna blow me kecks off.'

'Better out than in,' the greying lady behind the security glass with "Linda" on her name tag says. 'And it's gale force, not gay force.'

My still very sensitive stomach turns at the thought of someone else's irritable bowel as I recognise the voice and shameless abandon with which she's disclosing her ailments. This can be one person and one person only – Bunion Beryl. That's not her real name by the way, but I decided to use a pseudonym because I don't want her to feel bad if she ever reads this book.

'Me grandson Alby,' Beryl goes on, 'you know, the one who's just turned eight. He made me laugh t'other day.'

'What's he come out with this time?' asks Linda as she weighs an envelope.

'"Nana," he said, "do you know why they call it diarrhoea?" "No," I says to him. "Why do they call it diarrhoea?"'

'What d'he say?' Linda asks, holding a finger on the bridge of her big rimless glasses in suspense.

'"Well," he says. "They call it diarrhoea, Nana, cos it feels like you're dying in your rear."'

'He's a character him, int'he?' says Linda, shaking her head.

'He sent me video t'other day of him playing football,' Beryl says proudly, fishing out her phone from her coat pocket.

She holds the phone up to the security glass, presses play on a video, and shows Linda a clip of him juggling a football.

'Forty-odd keep me uppies he does 'ere, look,' she beams.

I want to correct her and say, 'Beryl, they're called Keepie Uppies, not Keep Me Uppies,' but I don't because I actually prefer "Keep Me Uppies." It sounds like a great name for a brand of erectile dysfunction drugs.

'Eh! You know I were talking t'other day about how to get me gravy fix on holiday?' Beryl carries on, back on the subject of runny brown liquid. 'I thought of a way to do it.'

'Go on,' Linda says, pressing a stamp onto the corner of an envelope.

'Gran-yoo-alls,' Beryl says, pointing at Linda through the security glass like she's cracked the code.

'Granules? Good idea, that!' Linda congratulates her. 'I'll 'aff do that next time we go away.'

In my early days up north, this would have been a scenario in which I would've made a disappearing act. I'd have made a surprised face as if to say, 'Bugger! I've forgotten to turn the oven off!' then run away, hidden around the corner and waited for Beryl to leave. Only then, when the coast was clear, would I have walked back in so I couldn't get trapped in a one-way conversation. Much like I did when I ran away from Beryl in Chapter 11, "Cold Pie, Warm Pasty", I'm ashamed to say.

But that was the old me. This is the new me. With my inner new-born Lancastrian child now piloting my behaviour. The same one who made me sit down and chat with the Rat Man and help me discover the gifts of new music, unexpected human connection and uplifting con-versation when I least expected it. That positive experience in mind, I remain firmly in line, even though I know Beryl could corner me at any moment like the first time we met in the woods. You never know, she might have some more health hacks like hairdryer-ing bunions.

'How's doggy?' asks Linda as she scoops up some coins Beryl has dropped into the tray for her.

'Who, Dennis?' Beryl checks. 'Same as always, still not weeing int' garden though,' she reports.

'Oh bloomin' 'eck. So what you doing?' Linda asks, sounding very concerned. 'He's not using your loo, is he?'

'No. Don't be daft. Luckily, someone threw a holly bush down our-wah ginnel[1] one night. It were all overt' shot.'

---

1. A space between two houses. Down south we'd call it an alley-way. 'Oop north they say ginnel.

I assume she means, all over the shop, not all over the shot, but I don't want to be rude and interrupt by correcting her.

'He likes t' wee on that instead. So, we teck him there before-wa bed.'

Beryl then turns around to me as I'm wondering if the conversation will eventually move on from piss and shit.

'Sorry for keeping you,' she apologises. 'I do go on a bit if you don't stop me.'

'Hello, Beryl,' I say, curious to know if she'll recognise me.

'Oh hello again. I've not seen you in quite a while,' she says.

'Yeah, I think it was about a year ago in the woods,' I reply.

'Were it that long ago? Bloomin' 'eck. How's Pearl?' she asks.

'Ah, you remembered her name,' I say. 'She's great, thanks.'

'Ooh, I could never forget that pretty little thing,' she says. 'How've you been?'

'I've been good, thanks,' I reply. 'Apart from having some terrible food poisoning that made me very ill.'

'Oh no,' she says. 'I've got irritable bowel, so I know how that feels to be on and off loo like a cat on a hot potato.'

'So I just heard,' I say, wondering if it's me that's been wrong all these years saying "cat on a hot tin roof."

'Are you better now?' she asks.

'Well,' I say in an everybody-gather-round-type tone, 'I thought I had salmonella poisoning. So I went to the doctors to give them a sample.'

'Stoo-wool sample?' Linda asks from behind the glass, finger on the bridge of her glasses again.

'Yep. A stool sample. But strangely, it came back clear,' I report. 'Which is weird because I was ill for months and until recently, I'd not been able to keep anything down apart from broccoli and sweet potatoes. Otherwise, you know?' I say, pointing to my back door.

'You felt like you were dying through your rear,' Beryl jokes.

'Exactly! But I'm definitely over the worst of whatever it was, thanks for asking.'

With no one else behind me in the queue, Beryl, Linda and I are free to carry on chatting.

'I basically lost two stone out of my backside,' I say to Beryl.

'Maybe that's what I need? A tummy bug to get rid of this lot,' she says, pinching at the love handles under her pink anorak. 'Slimming World's not been doing me much good,' she groans. 'But it's no use crying over split milk.'

'Spilt milk you mean, Beryl, love,' Linda says.

'Split milk, spilt milk, you know what I mean, don't you?' Beryl says. 'That's why I'm keeping up wit' line dancing. It's always been a happy humping ground for me.'

I zone out of the conversation for a moment and visualise Beryl humping unsuspecting people to American country music in the happy hunting ground of her line dancing classes. Maybe that's where the mad NISA shopkeeper first got into the bad habit of humping grannies?

'You look very tired,' Beryl says to me. 'Long weekend, worr'it?'

'My brother-in-law's wedding,' I reply. 'To say things got a little bit messy is an understatement. Too much of that,' I say, mock knocking back a pint glass.

'Ooh I don't drink much anymore, me,' she says. 'I'm on too much medication.'

'Neither do I,' I say, 'that's why I'm in such a mess.'

'One drink and I'm comatosed by me tablets.'

From my experiences as a teacher, I get the feeling that some form of dyslexia could be causing Beryl to constantly mix up her words and phrases.

I try to subliminally correct her without making her feel silly.

'Comatose?' I say.

'Yep, absolutely comatosed dabi-dosey,' Beryl says with a nod, then closes her eyes and honks a fake snore to get her point across.

'Even when we go on holiday, I don't drink a drop of the stuff.'

'That's very disciplined of you, Beryl,' I commend her.

'We just seem to spend all day playing that game. What's it called, Linda? The one where you fetch balls from't sandpit.'

Just as I'm about to tell her it's called "petanque", Beryl thinks she's got it.

'Kerplonk! That's what it's called.'

I try not to laugh while she continues.

'The only boner contender I have on me holidays is bloody flies.'

'Boner contender?' I say, stifling more laughter while imagining some weird television programme where a panel of judges are inspecting a line of erect penises (sponsored by Keep Me Uppies).

'Yep. Me only boner contender about going away is those bloomin' flies. I feel like I spend all'time squatting the bloomin' things.'

As Beryl's holidaying bone of contention comes to light and a middle-aged lady joins the queue behind me, I'm imagining Beryl squatting flies to death on poolside sun beds, crushing swarms of them with her backside as they buzz for mercy.

'And them bloomin' karaoke-cokey bars,' she says, going off on one. 'Make me want to cut me bloomin' ears off, they do. And don't talk to me about them taxis t'airport.'

There's no stopping her now.

'Cost an arm and leg these days.'

'You can get an Uber,' I suggest. 'They're a lot cheaper.'

'A hoover? What's a hoover gonna do for me?'

'He said "Uber," Beryl,' Linda says. 'You can get it on your phone to order a cheaper taxi. Henry bloomin' Hoover's not gonna drive you, is he? What are you like?'

'Oh I don't know. I'll 'aff get me son show me how it all works,' Beryl replies.

There's a rare silence in the conversation that's filled by the lady behind us talking on her mobile.

'She said she doesn't like onions,' the lady says to the person on the other end. 'Everybody likes onions. 'Ow can you not like onions? I just don't get it.'

'Well best be off. This lady's making me hungry talking about onions,' Beryl says, indicating the lady behind us. 'And, all I've had for me breakfast is hash brownies.'

Which could well have a lot more to do with the mixing of her words than the dyslexia.

Chapter 29

Batman and Robin

To entertain myself during those 50 days of lockdown in Tenerife, I decided to sniff out the pairs with holes from my sock drawer. While reluctantly accepting that it was time to part ways with my treasured avocado socks that I like to wear on my nights off, I heard Rachel cry out in distress. It was more a wail than a word. It was alarming. I bolted into the living room of our apartment fearing the worst.

'Matt's died,' she said quietly, her voice cracking with emotion.

'What?' I panicked, thinking it's my brother, Matt. 'Matt who?'

She sat on the sofa saying nothing, continuing to stare at a message on her phone as if in the hope that she'd misread it.

'Matt who, babe?' I rushed her for an answer.

'Matt,' she whimpered, palming tears off her cheeks. 'Matt Skirrow.'

'What? How?' I asked, still not really believing that what she was saying could possibly be true.

'Heart attack. Fell down dead in the kitchen.'

My entire body froze in shock as the reality bit down hard that one of our closest friends in Tenerife had just dropped dead.

Swallowing a lump in my throat, I had to blink tears out of my eyes to clear my blurred vision as Rachel got up from the sofa for a hug. We spent a long time sobbing in each other's arms.

When we eventually pulled ourselves together many toilet rolls later, our thoughts soon turned to his young family. This really couldn't have happened to nicer people. It was tragic. It was cruel. It was way too soon. At just 51 years young, Matt had left behind a heartbroken wife, a 21 year-old-son and a teenage daughter. Even now as I write in reflection, I still find it harrowing to think about.

Skiz (short for Skirrow), as his pals called him, was my man crush; my older brother from another mother. A role model for me in so many ways – a family man; a man's man; the best listener; always a shoulder to cry on; funny; even more hilarious and loveable when drunk; the life and soul of any party; adored by his wife and idolised by his lovely children. He was a traditional and proud Yorkshireman who grafted both day and night jobs to provide for his family.

Matt and I met in his night job where he worked as a stagehand in the dinner and dance show I joined as a cast member. The same one where Rachel and I met Roy Walker, the former host of the TV gameshow, Catchphrase, (remember the Roy Walker Roast in Chapter 5)? In that show I worked with Matt three evenings per week for five years and we soon became confidants after becoming colleagues. Rachel worked with him for three of those five years.

When, on my very first night that we worked together, I returned home to find he'd secretly filled my rucksack with rubbish from the backstage bins, I knew I'd found a partner in pranks and a friend for life. In revenge, I hid a dead cockroach in his mobile phone case. I still get weird looks from strangers when I burst out laughing remembering how he squealed in horror, then launched his phone the length of the backstage dressing room when he saw the cockroach in his hand.

Those 700-plus nights working with Matt were filled with laughter, classic backstage pranks and endless north-south banter.

'Don't fuck it up, you cockney tosser,' he'd whisper in my ears as I was about to go onstage.

'Go walk your whippet 'oop moors,' I'd hiss back.

Heartbreakingly, we were unable to pay our respects and celebrate Matt's life in the conventional way because of lockdown restrictions. To this very day, nearly two years since heaven recruited an angel of the north, Rachel and I feel it's a wrong we have yet to put right. So, that's why we've decided to walk the Leeds to Liverpool Canal backwards. I don't mean moonwalking Michael Jackson style, I mean walking towards, instead of from, Leeds, Matt's hometown. Our plan when we arrive in Leeds after a week-long, cross-country trek on foot, is to pay homage to Matt by laying some flowers at the canal side quay. To finally say our own personal and long overdue goodbye.

With only a week free between Christmas Day and having to go back to our jobs after the New Year, we don't have enough time to walk all 127 miles of the canal. So, instead of starting in Liverpool, we jumped on a train in Bolton, jumped off in Blackburn and started walking from there.

We've passed through Burnley, where the smell of curry from the rows of terraced housing along the canal teased our perpetual hiker's hunger. In Clayton-le-Moors, a reported site of regular paranormal activity, we picked up the pace, having the spooky feeling we were being chased by ghosts. In the village of Barnoldswick, we arrived after dark after having been soaked to our rainy bones, then found a B&B that very strangely had paintings of rabbits everywhere in our room. Whilst I sat on the toilet, I had one looking at me, ears aloft on the bathroom wall as I unloaded some pellets. There was even a rabbit portrait on my bedside table watching me as I tried to fall asleep. It took me ages to nod off because I was worried that Thumper would nibble on my carrot during the night.

Between Blackburn and Leeds, we've battled wind, rain and hail; sleet, snow and hissing swans. We've strode through rainbows spanning the horizon. We've plodded along cobbled paths, boggy bridleways and slippery slush. We've passed under no less than 122 granite stone bridges and conquered 75 miles in seven days. I would like it to be known and noted that I've worn shorts for every single one of those 75 ball-freezing miles. On the lower half of my body I'm officially a northerner. On the top half, however, I have to admit that I'm still a southerner because I've been wearing more coats than a nightclub cloakroom can handle.

This winter adventure, strolling east to west across Northern England, has far exceeded our expectations. It's treated us to some sensory delights that will live in our memories forever: the rolling, golf-course-green Yorkshire Dales climbing the skies like a picture perfect scene from an illustrated fairytale; the smell of lemony detergent from the clothes drying on washing lines in the gardens of the houses down by the water; the sound of ducks splashing in the canal when they come in to land, mingling with birdsong. Sheep, cows and goats grazing and bleating in the open fields accompanying the canal almost all the way.

Some of the characters we've come across in the last week have had us laughing ourselves to sleep. Early one morning, a group of young fishermen in the town of Apperley Bridge near Bradford saw Rachel and me in our ponchos trying to prevent the rain from flying in our faces. With our pointy triangular hoods, cutting very unusual figures, we could have easily been mistaken by the youths for members of a satanic cult.

'What the fook?' one of them blurted out when he saw us walking towards them at sunrise. Fishing rods in hands, their eyes widened in bewilderment as we approached.

'It's fooking Batman and Robin,' another lad said, clocking our ponchos flailing behind us in the wind like superhero capes.

'What fook are you two up to?' another very politely asked.

'Walking to Leeds from Blackburn,' I shouted back over the rain.

'Eh? Why fook would you do that?'

'I'm taking a pair of pants back to Primark that don't fit me,' I replied to confuse them even more. I guessed that they probably wouldn't want to hear the real reason.

'Proper fooking mad 'eads!' another lad said, taking a drag of a cigarette.

It was only then that it dawned on me that we must be the only two people up north who think it would be fun to roam across the country on foot in the depths of winter.

On our penultimate day, we bumped into an old Yorkshireman in a flat cap, raincoat and wellies for whom our escapades were much less of a big deal.

'Ow long you two been walking then?' he asked, standing right in front of us on the muddy towpath so we had no choice but to stop.

'About seven hours so far today,' I said.

'Aye,' he dismissed with a nonchalant nod, like he'd have been more impressed if we'd said 16. 'You doing the lot?' he asked, tucking his waterproof trousers into his muddy green wellies.

'Almost,' I replied. 'We started walking from Blackburn. Keighley's been my favourite so far,' I said, talking up the small town. 'The curry was amazing.'

'Where?' he asked.

'Keighley. Best masala I've ever had.' I showed him a picture on my phone. Of the town on my maps app, not the curry.

'That's not how you say it!' he ridiculed me.

'Really?'

'You don't want to go around spouting off like that. People will think you're an immigrant or summat. Get it right!' he said. 'It's Keith-ly. You pronounce the "gh" like a "th".'

'Oh,' I said, wondering how I was supposed to know that since I don't live around here.

Then the red mist came over me. What the bloody hell did he mean by that last comment, "immigrant or summat"?

I bit my tongue for a moment and considered my response. My first thought was to rebuke his stupid racist face, but then I remembered how the young lad in Chapter 17 dealt with nearly being smashed into by that van; how he managed to make light of a potentially dark situation by cracking a joke to deescalate. Surprising myself, I climb down off my high horse and do the same.

'I'm from down south so I might as well be an immigrant up here, the way I talk,' I said to defuse the situation.

There. No precious energy wasted on a narrow-minded idiot, and another sign of how the people up north, that young car driver in particular, have been a good influence on me.

'Well done,' Rachel said as we left him behind and walked on into the driving rain. 'I thought you were going to let loose on him then.'

'No point,' I said. 'As the saying goes, you can't teach an old racist fool new tricks.'

Just like that bigoted idiot, the boat traffic signs in Yorkshire didn't pull any punches either. They didn't just say "Slow" as they did in Lancashire; they commanded the boats to go "DEAD SLOW!"

While Yorkshire folk are well known for their directness, they're also famously hospitable. Sabine Baring Gould (1834–1924), a novelist who hailed from Devon, couldn't agree more. He once reflected: *"I look back with the greatest pleasure at the kindness and hospitality that I was met with during some of the happiest years of my life in Yorkshire."*

Rachel and I had a similar experience in a pub in Sealsden. When we fell through the door looking like we'd been on a polar expedition, a hospitable barmaid ran from behind the bar, pulled out some chairs by the fireside for us and popped a couple of logs on the fire. To the crackle of firewood, we got the hot coffee she made us into our frozen bodies. In North Yorkshire in Skipton, a town recently championed by *The Sunday Times* as the Best Place to Live in the UK, we got jolly, spirit-lifting hellos from every single person we came across – dog walkers, runners and people living on the barges alike. It was the perfect way at sunrise to begin our new year. When we stopped in a café at Bingley's spectacular Five Rise Locks, a local gave us a laugh when he saw us walk in with our big backpacks and sung to us the famous song from *Snow White and the Seven Dwarves*, 'Hiiiiiii-hooooo!'

***

Walking the final hour of the seventh day of our adventure traversing the back of the northern beyond, Rachel and I are re-living all these memories on our approach into Leeds.

Signs of big city life are now rife: overfilled bins spilling coffee cups, nappies and crumpled cigarette boxes onto the towpath; canal bridges that in the countryside were decorated with Mother Nature's moss are now daubed in urban graffiti (Nat has herpes, by the way); the melody of water running into the canal from the rivers flowing adjacent has been drowned out by local trains and high-speed locomotives rattling around rails crisscrossing the suburbs.

When we finally reach the quayside in Leeds where cafés, restaurants and plush modern apartments overlook the canal, Rachel goes to warm up in a café while I go find somewhere to buy some flowers.

In a Sainsbury's just around the corner, I choose a big bunch of white roses. I figure they couldn't be any more fitting since it's the same flower on the badge of Matt's beloved football team, Leeds United.

Early afternoon, Rachel and I make our way to a sign post marking the official beginning of the Leeds to Liverpool Canal. We lay down the white roses on a bed of grass, then silently say our personal goodbyes to the sound of a kayaker's oars gracefully stroking the water's surface.

Telling Rachel I need a moment to myself, I walk up the canal to a wooden footbridge crossing over the water where a current is flowing upstream. I take one white rose with me. Standing in the middle of the bridge, I drop the rose into the canal, then watch it float off in the direction of Liverpool, 127 miles away. As the white rose drifts ever so slowly but surely away from me in the brown water, I have a strong feeling that, as crazy as it sounds, while I can still see it Matt and I are somehow magically together again, and he's still alive. Although I know the rose will wither and perish long before it reaches Liverpool, I let my imagination take over.

I dream of the rose making it all the way to Merseyside where it's delivered to the Irish Sea, then given a send-off into the infinity of the Atlantic Ocean where it'll live forever. Just like I believe Matt's kind, beautiful and bright soul will do. As I continue to gaze at the white rose spinning like a clock hand in the water as it's being carried away,

I think about how he'd be laughing at me trying to adapt to life up north. He'd love it that after all my mocking of his northern accent, the local dialect is tumbling out of my mouth on a regular basis; that I've started calling ladies "love", dinner, "tea", and sandwiches, "butties"; that I'm even having butter in my crispy bacon butties.

Matt would be proud of me that I've dropped my trousers, my long johns are long gone, and, like the locals, I'm now wearing shorts outside in winter; that I've learned how to order a meat and potato pasty without ending up with a pie in my face.

As the wooden bridge I'm standing on shakes to the thudding blades of a low-flying police helicopter, I wonder if he'd believe me that I'm line dancing with Lancashire grannies in aid of Bolton Hospice. That I've even adorned the football shirt of a northern team and sung their songs. Matt would definitely have preferred, however, that the white rose of Leeds United crossed my heart instead of Bolton's red rose.

What I do know for sure is that Matt would find it highly amusing that I've gone from being scared to say hello to strangers, to being comfortable going into great details about my ailments with them, as I did with Beryl and Linda in the post office when I told them I was dying through my rear. He'd be bowled over to know that as well as saying those cheerful hellos to strangers, I'm also sitting down to say long goodbyes with them over tea and biscuits, just like I did with Rat Man.

'I know I'm "not from round 'ere" as people keep telling me, Matt,' I say to the swirling black clouds, hoping he can somehow hear me. 'But at least now I feel like I fit in.'

As I'm about to walk away from the bridge and back to Rachel at the quayside, an apparition of Matt enshrouded in divine light appears in the black clouds.

'So you think you're one of us now, do you?' he asks, popping a flat cap onto his head of wispy blond hair.

'What can I say, Matt? Your fellow northerners have made me more open, more laid back, more human. They've brought out the best in me. Just like our friendship brought the best out of me.'

'Stop being such a soft southern Jessie, you cockney tosser,' Matt says with a wink while raising a pint.

'Rest in mushy Yorkshire peas, Skiz.' I salute him.

Before You Go...

If you've enjoyed *Not From Round Here*, I'd be so grateful if you could write me a five star review on Amazon. It'll help me shift a few more copies and save up enough money to buy a new big coat.

You can do so by clicking this link below if you think the book merits such praise.

https://www.amazon.com/review/create-review/error?&asin=B0 CVG1ZKMN

If you liked this book, you might also be interested in my first, bestselling book, *The Only Way Is West*.

Here's the link if you'd like to read it or listen to the audiobook version:

mybook.to/amazonbestseller

One last thing before you skedaddle...

If the thought of keeping in touch fills you with glee, head on over to my website.

On there I'll tell you how you can see some photos from my life 'oop north as well as other exciting stuff like some clips of my attempts at moving into stand up comedy.

Go on... I dare you. Just log onto www.bradleychermside.com

Meet you there!

Acknowledgements

Thousand thanks to my developmental editor and fellow Essexonian Suzy K. Quinn for helping me to renew my belief in this project when I doubted it was worth carrying on with.

Thanks to my copy editor Quinn Nichols for some truly exceptional work in helping me to get the manuscript ready for publication.

Last but certainly not least, thanks to the people of the north of England, Bolton and Westhoughton in particular, for your charm, wit and humour; for making the ordinary in everyday life extraordinarily entertaining.

Printed in Great Britain
by Amazon